PAMELA NOTTINGHAM

Bedfordshire Lace Making

B.T. Batsford Ltd · London

Acknowledgements

I appreciate very much the help and encouragement that I receive from my husband, Arthur Johnson, and again thank him for his patience and skill in producing all the illustrations.

As a lacemaker I have made many friends in Britain and throughout the world and I should like to thank them for their interest and enthusiasm.

ISBN 0 7134 5181 5

A catalogue record for this book is available from the British Library

Printed in Great Britain
by BPCC Hazells Ltd
Member of BPCC Ltd
for the Publisher
B.T. Batsford Ltd
4 Fitzhardinge Street
London W1H 0AH

Contents

Preface

Bedfordshire lace was made throughout the East Midlands in the second half of the nineteenth century. For many years the lacemakers had worked Bucks Point lace but the development of machines capable of producing lace brought dismay and anxiety not only to the lacemakers but also to the manufacturers and dealers. The Great Exhibition of 1851 had a tremendous influence on English bobbin lace. Many new patterns were designed and existing Bucks Point patterns re-grounded with plaits, picots and leaves. The resulting lace, very much influenced by the laces of Malta, was known as Bedfordshire Maltese lace. Designers, notably Thomas Lester of Bedford, attended all the international exhibitions in Europe; he returned with medals and commendations for his entries and a wealth of ideas gleaned from studying other exhibits. Design features, for example the flowers of Belgian needlepoint lace, were incorporated into new designs . . . they did not lend themselves readily to bobbin lace and were a real challenge to the lacemakers! Always looking for new ideas, the designers took the fillings of Honiton lace to become the grounds of Bedfordshire, and re-introduced as fillings honeycomb and point ground, the traditional stitches of the East Midland laces. In the past, the workers made square leaves but today the lacemaker prefers to make pointed leaves.

Although one strives for perfection it should be remembered that close detail is rarely seen when an article is in use. Several countries have traditional plaited laces but each has developed its own special characteristics.

Lace was taught either in the lace school or as a skill handed on from mother to daughter. There were no manuals or written instructions, indeed few people could read. Information was passed on verbally and when the lacemaker interpreted her pattern the chief considerations were appearance and durability sufficient to satisfy the dealer who purchased the lace, and also speed as she needed to earn her livelihood.

As one studies old lace and recognizes the much-used traditional methods, occasional deviation in technique will be found. Surely one cannot say that the lace was badly made? It would be more appropriate to question why the method was adopted and consider its value. Was it a local innovation? . . . One will never know! If it satisfies a need why should it not be used again? For example, lace with the trail retaining the same number of pairs throughout, with leaves and plaits travelling through in the Cluny manner, is sometimes seen. The technique is less usual and therefore the method should be used with discretion. The lacemaker today will probably have experience of a range of lace types and may introduce a variety of techniques to improve the appearance. However, the true Bedfordshire lacemaker will use traditional methods unless it is to the detriment of the lace. Honiton fillings used as grounds or fillings may be worked in the Devon or Bedfordshire manner. For example, the ground which is similar to the Honiton blossom filling is today frequently worked in the Honiton manner, whereas in the past it was worked quite differently (refer to diagram 162). Bedfordshire lace designs are known for their flowers, leaves and plaits. A dominant feature in most patterns is the cloth stitch trail, which serves two purposes: it enhances the design and it is a means of taking pairs from one part of the pattern to another.

A lacemaker should have a knowledge of Bedfordshire lace before attempting to 'tidy' or 'true' an old pricking. Pattern drafts are accurate but many of the old prickings need attention. Bedfordshire lace is not geometric, and the variations and discrepancies are an individuality to be treasured, not removed for fear of imperfection. To move a gently flowing trail so that it drops to the footside to avoid long twisted weavers is incorrect. From a distance the line of the trail is all-important and the twisted threads are unnoticed. Plaits in ground usually travel in a straight line and should enter the design feature maintaining the same line. Sometimes this results in differences from head to head, perhaps caused by inaccurate pricking, but the final appearance is more important than looking closely to count the pinholes between plaits! Many traditional edgings were made continuously and have no corners. Occasionally, a modern adaptation is successful but too often the character of the design is lost. An old fine linen handkerchief has a special beauty in lace gently gathered around the corners. Adaptation and alteration are essential to suit late-twentieth-century needs but there is a need to work with sympathy and understanding.

Introduction

Most of the patterns, apart from the drafts in the last section, were acquired in South Buckinghamshire, where they had been worked at the turn of the century or earlier. Usually I have reproduced them the same size as the original; however, some will be more attractive if the pricking is reduced.

I am assuming the lacemaker has a knowledge of the two basic stitches – cloth (or whole) stitch and half stitch – and an understanding of the preparation necessary to begin a piece of lace. Section One contains very simple and quick-to-work plaited laces that will ensure that the student new to Bedfordshire lace has adequate practice at leaves, plaits and picots. Sections Two and Three offer a gradual introduction to Bedfordshire techniques, and in Section Four is a selection of patterns which includes Bucks Point and honeycomb grounds. Section Five offers a range of patterns including collars, cuffs and yokes. The last six patterns are an introduction to the edgings and insertions from the pattern drafts of Lester, Clarke, Allen and Marshall. These interesting designs, classed as Bedfordshire lace, are worthy of recognition in their own right as a major lace of the East Midlands.

Techniques are grouped at the beginning of each section and the detailed index ensures easy reference.

The problem of how and where to begin is dealt with as a general point in Pattern 11 on page 40. Certain patterns are given full instructions but to avoid unnecessary repetition the lacemaker should, for other patterns, apply the principles stated and advice given elsewhere.

The reproduction of large prickings on a page of limited size is always a problem and it is difficult to match pricking pieces together accurately. Large patterns are reduced, and the correct size can be achieved on a photocopier with enlargement facility. The scale accompanies each pricking.

Pattern interpretation

The ink lines used to indicate plaits, leaves and picots are shown clearly in the patterns in this book. However, old patterns have many and varied markings.
Refer to Pricking 1.

(a) Short black lines indicate plaits; the lines may be marked directly to a pinhole or to the side. A line slightly above the hole indicates that the plait will be taken in at the hole and the line below indicates that the plait is left out at the pinhole.

(b) Small rings around holes indicate picots; note that there are picots on the headside but these are accepted without the additional marking.

(c) The leaf

(d) Small rings around holes in the centre of design features indicate raised tallies.

(e) Single or double lines indicate weaver crossing.

(*f*) Small cross indicates the use of half stitch.

(*g*) This ink line indicates a trail.

(*h*) Continuous lines may indicate the use of gimp threads or possibly the indication of the feature without the use of gimp.

NOTE: Plaits and leaves may be drawn between pinholes. This indicates that the pairs will be brought in at the next hole (the weaver works through them before the pin is placed), or that the pairs will be left out below the pin (after the pin has been covered and the weaver continued across the lace).

Preparation of pricking

The traditional method, and still the most successful, is to prick the pattern onto glazed card or vellum and mark in the features with permanent ink. It is achieved as follows:

(*a*) Take the copy, plain white paper and card in that order and fasten them firmly to a pricking board with *four drawing pins*.

(*b*) Prick the footside, using a ruler to ensure a straight edge.

(*c*) Prick the pattern, but do not prick in the picots until the plaits have been drawn in.

(*d*) Mark in the ink lines using a fine pen and waterproof ink.

The drawing pins may be removed, whenever and as often as the lacemaker wishes, in order to mark the design on paper and card. It is easy to reassemble copy/paper/card and, using the pricker, check that they are together accurately.

Always mark in the same features on all pattern repeats at the same time. Hold the copy/paper/card to the light to check that all holes have been made. The paper copy is an exact replica of the pricking and more useful for reference than a photocopy, which may be slightly different.

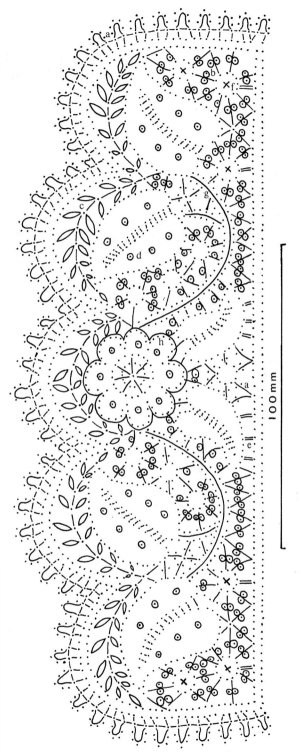

Figure 1

The above method is no longer favoured by many lacemakers, who prefer to glue the paper copy onto card and either colour it or cover it with transparent adhesive plastic. In which case it is essential that:

(a) The copy is securely fastened to the card.
(b) The colour allows the holes and threads to be easily seen and is restful to the eyes.
(c) All holes should be pricked with the pricking on a flat surface *before* lace making commences.
(d) Holes must be pricked *accurately* as a black dot and a black hole on a fine pricking may be seen as two holes.

All methods are time consuming, but care is necessary to achieve an understanding of the method and good lace results.

Threads

There is a wide variety of threads available today, but only linen will produce the crisp firm plaits and picots so characteristic of this lace. In the past much lace was made in cotton thread as the workers found it easier to use; however quality lace was always made in linen. The tension, personal preference, and the smoothness of the thread all contribute to the result.

Threads can be categorized into four groups, the middle two being most used for general work. However, this is only a guide and it is advisable to work a small section of the pattern – the footside or a trail and some plaits – to confirm suitability. The numbering of threads from different manufacturers varies, and indeed variations of any one thread may occur over a period of time.

Group 1: any linen thread from 35/2 to 80/2, i.e. coarse thread of varying thickness; the smaller the number the thicker the thread.

Group 2: Bockens 90/2, 100/2 linen thread, Madeira Tanne 30 and D.M.C. Retors d'Alsace 30 (also known as Broder Machine) are comparable.

Group 3: 100/3 Brok, Madeira Tanne 50, D.M.C. Retors d'Alsace 50 are comparable.

Group 4: 140/2 linen thread, Madeira Tanne 80, Brok 120/3 or 100/2.

NOTE: 100 Bouc linen and 60/2 Brok cotton are useful as they fall between Groups 2 and 3.

Linen thread will produce a crisp firm result and is preferable. Unfortunately, at the present time, fine linen thread is unavailable.

Gimp thread: D.M.C. Coton Perlé nos. 8 and 12.

Pins

0.53 diameter pins are suitable for use with threads in Groups 3 and 4. A thicker pin, diameter 0.67, is preferable when using heavier thread. Pins should be left along the footside edge and holding the headside picots for as long as possible. They should be removed one at a time and if necessary the lace should be held in position on the pricking with a long pin or needle pin.

NOTE: The right side of the completed lace is usually the underside, i.e. that which is against the pricking card. However, it is more convenient to work raised tallies and flat leaves on the upper side which consequently becomes the right side.

1

Plaited and Cluny Laces

Techniques for basic patterns

The footside

The number and arrangement of passive pairs may vary but the footside always has a straight edge; this is achieved by alternating the weaver pairs. The passive pairs may be twisted or worked in cloth stitch; the latter is more common in older patterns. Passive and weaver pairs are used in a variety of ways to achieve a neat corner at 90°.

Plaits

The plait is made using two pairs of bobbins working continuous half stitch. Refer to Fig 2.

Figure 2

It is necessary to pull each stitch firmly to ensure a flat and closely woven plait. The correct length is important to achieve a straight and crisp result.

Plaits with more than two pairs

Work from right to left through all pairs in half stitch. Continue working from right to left in half stitch, pulling the plait into position at the end of each row. The outside threads will be used to make picots in the normal manner.

Alternatively a plait may be made using two threads as one (i.e. six threads worked as two singles and two doubles or eight threads worked as four doubles). Picots are always made using two threads only.

Picots

These are worked on one or both sides of a plait for decoration. Normally picots are made with two threads but if the thread is thick a single thread picot is more satisfactory.

Picot on the left side: Fig. 3 a and b

Take the two left-hand threads of the plait and twist three or five times. Take a pin in the right hand and hold it – point to the left – over the extreme left thread. Bring the point under the thread towards the worker and over into the picot hole. Keep it *loosely* round the pin. Take

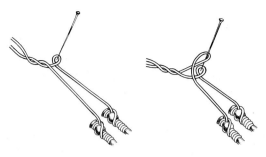

| Figure 3a | Figure 3b | Figure 4a | Figure 4b |

the other thread to the front and round the pin in a clockwise direction. Twist the threads together three times and pull together. They should form a twisted cord around the pin.

If the threads remain as two separate rings the picot must be remade. To avoid this ensure that the two loops around the pin remain *very loose* until all the twists are made.

Picot on the right side: Fig. 4 a and b

Twist the two right-hand threads of the plait three or five times. Take a pin in the right hand and hold it – point towards the left – under the right thread, bring the point over the thread towards the worker, and into the picot hole. Take the other thread and bring it in front and behind in an anticlockwise direction. Twist the threads three times and pull together firmly.

Picots using thick thread: Fig. 5

Take the two left-hand threads of the plait in the left hand and hold them taut. Take a pin in the right hand, put it under the right thread and pull the left thread across under it (*a*). Bring the point of the pin towards the worker over the crossed threads, then turn the point away and under the threads and up between them (*b*). Put the pin into the hole on the left of the plait (*c*) or to the right of the plait (*d*). Manipulate the threads until a single tight picot appears on the side of the plait.

Picots on both sides

When the first picot has been completed make one half stitch before working the second. This avoids an ugly hole between picots.

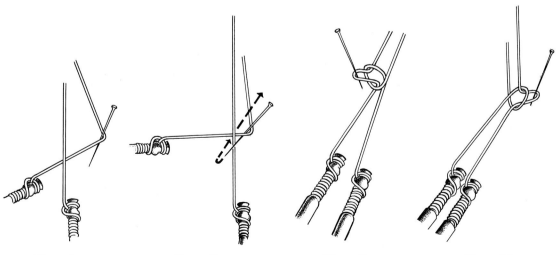

| Figure 5a | Figure 5b | Figure 5c | Figure 5d |

Leaves

Practice is essential to master this technique, and to achieve success one should choose a pattern with many leaves!

Refer to Fig. 6. Make a cloth (whole) stitch, pulling it evenly and closely. Allow the bobbins to lie on the pillow. Take the third thread to the right under and over the outside thread. Continue to weave under the centre thread and over and under the left-hand thread, over the centre thread and under the right-hand thread. Hold the weaving thread throughout.

the weaving thread to lie snugly around the threads. The centre thread requires little or no attention at this stage. At first shape the leaf from the point, ensuring that it is wide enough to look attractive. It is unnecessary to reduce the width until at least three-quarters of the leaf has been worked. Complete it with cloth stitch.

A leaf requires support until it is taken into the work; either put a pin between the pairs using any convenient hole or lay the weaver thread back over the work until required. Practice is essential in achieving a pleasing result.

Figure 6

Figure 7

The shape of the leaf is controlled by the outside threads and its evenness by the weaving thread. Hold the weaving bobbin between the first finger and thumb of the right hand and either hold the right-hand bobbin between third and fourth fingers or keep the side of the hand on it to prevent it from moving. Incline the left thread to the side to control the width of the leaf and manoeuvre

Square leaves are occasionally required and these are made similarly. Refer to Fig. 7. Twist each pair twice, keep the side threads well apart and weave the leaf. Twist each pair twice to complete it. *It is important to work the pair without the weaver thread into the work first as any tension on the weaver thread will distort the shape.*

Raised leaves (sometimes called raised tallies)

The weaver stays at the edge of the feature. Centre pairs – or whichever are appropriate – work a square leaf and the threads are taken back over a pin (refer to Fig. 8) and then pulled gently so that the leaf curls up and backwards over the pin. Work a half stitch with these pairs before taking the weaver across the lace. Raised tallies may be worked over cloth or half stitch. The visible surface of the lace on the pillow is usually considered to be the right side when making a pattern with raised tallies.

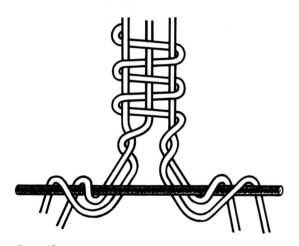

Figure 8

Flat leaves over cloth or half stitch

A pin is placed between two pairs – not the weaver – and these are laid back for the leaf. The work is continued to the position of the end of the leaf. The two leaf pairs are brought back into position and the leaf is made; a pin is put in to hold it in position. Weaving continues including the leaf pairs. When two leaves make a crossing over cloth or half stitch, leave out the necessary pairs, work to the crossing and work it, trapping one pair with a passive thread. This ensures that the crossing remains in the correct position.

Crossings

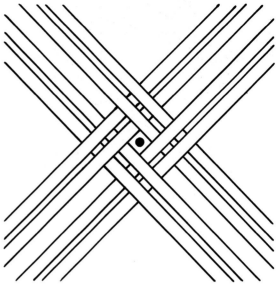

Figure 9

The four-plait crossing: Fig. 9

The four pairs come from two plaits or leaves. Regard each pair as a single thread and work a cloth stitch with the pin in the centre (i.e. cross, twist, pin, cross).

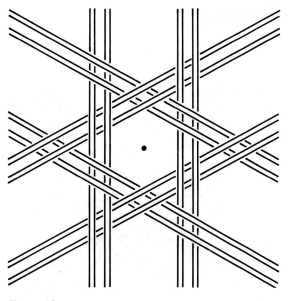

Figure 10

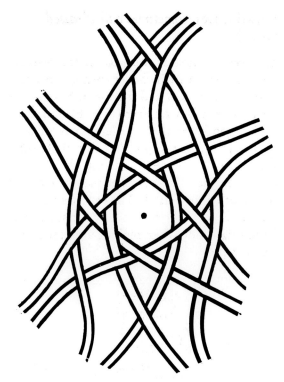

Figure 11

The six-plait crossing: Fig. 10

Use the three plaits/leaves as six pairs.

Take the right centre pair over the next pair to the right.

Take the left centre pair under the next pair to the left.

Cross the new centre pairs right over left and pin between them.

Take the pair to the right of the pin out to the right over and under the pairs.

Take the left centre pair out to the left under and over the pairs.

Take the left centre pair under the next pair to the left.

Take the right centre pair over the next pair to the right.

Cross the new centre pairs right over left.

Take the right centre pair over the next pair to the right.

Take the left centre pair under the next pair to the left.

The eight-plait crossing: Fig. 11

Use the four plaits/leaves as eight pairs, keeping each pair together and using as a single thread throughout.

Centre four pairs work half stitch.

The right-hand four pairs work half stitch.

The left-hand four pairs work half stitch.

Repeat these three moves.

Put up a pin between the centre pairs. The centre four pairs work cloth stitch.

Using the left-hand four pairs, cross centre-left over centre-right.

Using the right-hand four pairs, cross centre-left over centre-right.

Pattern 1   Figs 12, 13 and 14

8 pairs. D.M.C. Broder Machine no. 30, or
Bockens Linen 100/2

Footside Hang two pairs *round* pin A, twist
each pair three times – this forms a twisted
cord behind the pin. Cover with cloth stitch
and two twists on each pair. Give the
outside pair one twist extra (three
altogether). Ignore the outer pair and work
cloth stitch and twist through two pairs
hung *side by side* on pin *a*. Twist the weaver
twice more and put up pin B to the right of
it. Work the weaver to the footside edge (to
the right) with cloth stitch and twist
through the two passive pairs. Twist it once
more and work through the last pair with
cloth stitch and two twists. Again give the
outside pair one twist extra and put up pin
C to the left of *both* pairs. Ignore the outer
pair and return to D with cloth stitch and
twist through the passive pairs.

Plaits and picots Hang two pairs *round* each
of pins *b* and *c*. As these pairs will normally
arrive at the pin as plaits, they are ready to
make the first four-plait crossing at pin E.
Remove pins *b* and *c* and pull the pairs
down into position. Make a plait from E to
D. Take the weaver from the footside and
work cloth stitch through both plait pairs,
twist the weaver twice and put in pin D to
the right of the weaver. Take the weaver
back to the right through the plait pairs in
cloth stitch. Twist it once before working
cloth and twist through two passive pairs,
twist the weaver once more and work cloth
stitch and two twists on the outside edge.
Put up the pin which is in the same position
as pin A – the beginning of the work.
Remove pin *a* and ease the passive pairs
into position.

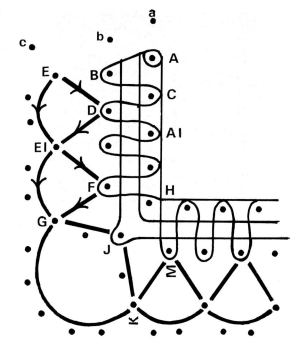

Figure 12

The pairs at E plait to E1 making two picots
on the left side of the plait on the way. The
plait pairs at D plait to E1. A four-plait
crossing is made at E1. A complete repeat
has been worked.

The corner The weaver at F works back to
the footside and corner pin H is put in
position. Plait from G to J working one
picot on the left side. The left passive pair
temporarily acts as weaver and works cloth
stitch through the plait pairs from G. Put in
pin J to the right of this weaver and weave
back through these pairs. Plait to K working
the picot on the left side. Plait from G to K
making picots, work the four-plait crossing
at K. The footside weaver works as usual
through the passive pairs in cloth stitch and
twist and on through the plait from K in
cloth stitch to M.

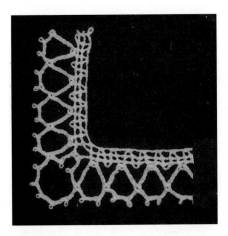

Figure 13

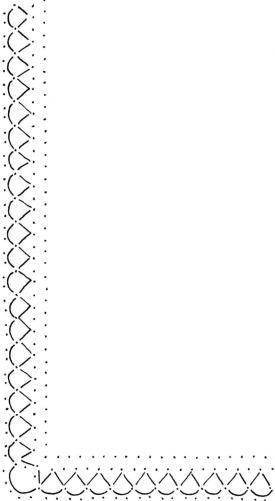

Figure 14

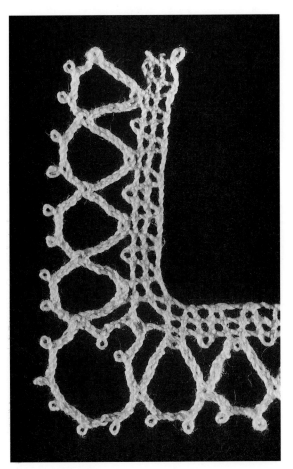

Figure 13 (detail)

Pattern 2 Figs 15, 16 and 17

8 pairs, D.M.C. Broder Machine no. 30 or
Bockens Linen 100/2

This pattern is very similar to Pattern 1 but
there are leaves instead of plaits and
additional picots. The instructions for
letters A – E apply to both patterns. Leaves
and picots are worked according to the
diagram.

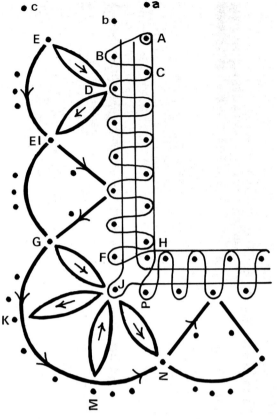

Figure 16

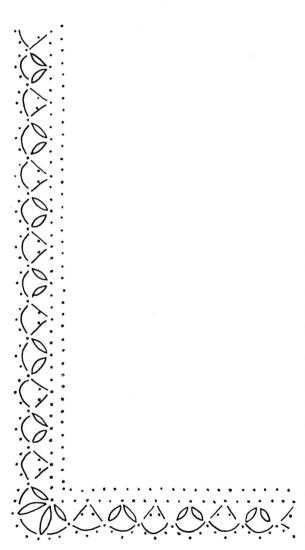

Figure 15

The corner The use of the passives and
weaver is similar to pattern 1. Work from F
to corner pin H. The left passive works
cloth stitch through the leaf pairs from G
and pin J is put up to the right of it. Weave
back through leaf pairs only and leave the
temporary weaver in this position. Make a
leaf to K and work the four-plait crossing.
The four pairs plait with picots to M.
Work a four-plait crossing at M and make
the leaf to J. Remove pin J and use the
temporary weaver at the pin to work
through the leaf pairs from M. Replace pin
J and work back through the leaf pairs. The
temporary weaver becomes the passive pair
again and the other pairs make the leaf to
N. The weaver at corner pin H works
through the passives to P and back to the
footside. The corner is complete.

Figure 17

Pattern 3   Figs 18, 19 and 20

8 pairs, Bockens linen thread 100/2

Footside This is similar to Patterns 1 and 2 but the passive pairs are untwisted. Work from A to D as follows:
Hang two pairs round pin A and twist each pair three times. Cover with cloth stitch and two twists on each pair; give the outside pair one twist extra. Ignore the outer pair and work cloth stitch back through two pairs hung on a pin at *a*. Twist the weaver three times and put up pin B to the right of it. Work back to the footside through two pairs in cloth stitch. Twist the weaver twice and work cloth stitch and two twists on the outside edge. Give the outer pair one twist extra and put up pin C to the left of both pairs. Ignore the outer pair and work back through two passive pairs with cloth stitch.

Plaits and picots The arrangement of plaits and picots in this pattern is known as 'Ninepin'; it is the traditional headside edging on many Bedfordshire patterns. Hang two pairs in order on pin *b*; the weaver from the footside at D works cloth stitch through these two pairs. Put in pin D to the right of the weaver which returns to the footside at A1. Remove pin *b* and pull the pairs down for a plait which is made to pin E. Replace pin *b* and hang two more pairs *round* it. Use these and the plait pairs to make a plait crossing at E. Remove pin *b* and pull the pairs into position. Plait the right-hand pairs to pin J. Plait the left-hand pairs with picots at F, G and H to J. Make a four-plait crossing at J. Plait the right-hand pairs to D1 and the left-hand pairs for the next ninepin plait. One pattern repeat is complete.

NOTE: To achieve a close neat plait, it is necessary to plait from G in a continuous line from F and then to incline it to position H for the picot.

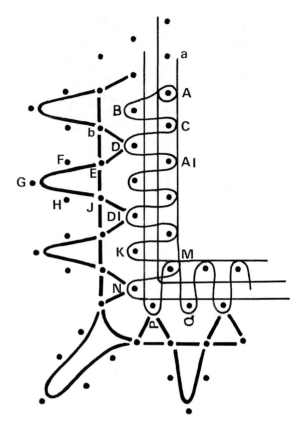

Figure 18

The corner This illustrates an alternative method of using passive pairs to achieve a neat corner. Work from K to the corner pin, put in pin M to the left of the weaver but do *not* make the outside edge stitch. Twist the weaver twice and work through the passive and plait pairs, put in pin N and work back through plait pairs and the left passive pair only. Work plaits and picots from N to P. Use the left passive pair to work cloth stitch through the plait pairs. Put up pin P and weave back to the corner pin M through the plait pairs and two passive pairs. Twist the weaver twice, remove pin M and work the edge stitch (cloth and two twists and the extra twist on the outside pair). Replace the pin to the left of these pairs. Ignore the outer pair and work to Q. Continue.

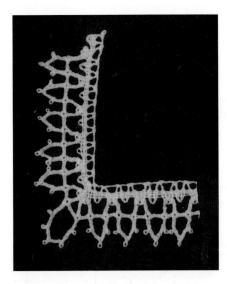

Figure 19

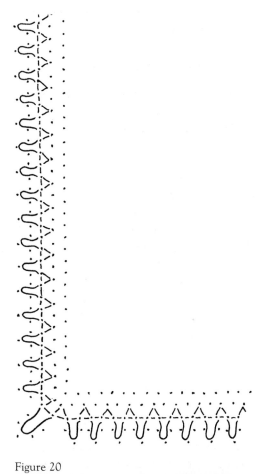

Figure 20

Figure 19 (detail)

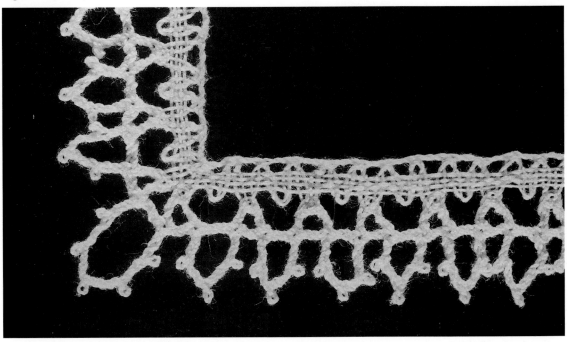

Pattern 4 Figs 21, 22 and 23

10 pairs, 100/2 linen thread

Begin at A, work through two passive pairs
with cloth stitch and twist and through two
pairs with cloth stitch for the first plait to
C. At C and D add pairs at four-plait
crossings.

The corner The weaver from the corner pin
N, worked as in previous pattern, works
back to P and returns through plait and

passive pairs to become the inner passive
pair. From the crossing at Q the right pairs
are plaited back to R, the outer passive
weaves through them, and the plait is made
to S. The original inner passive works cloth
and twist through the outer passive and
cloth stitch through the plait pairs from S at
pin T. It works back through these four
pairs to complete corner pin N. Plaits from
S and T work to crossing U.

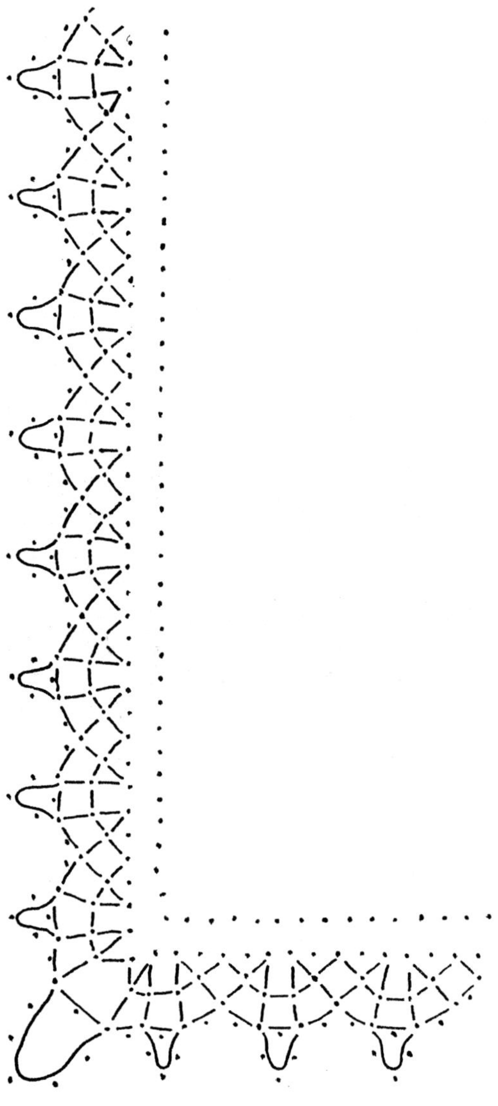

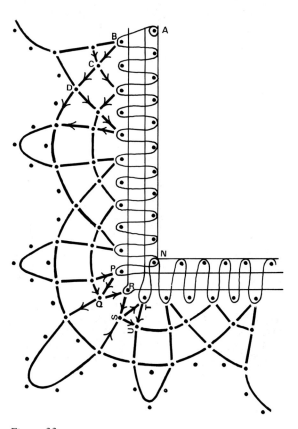

Figure 22

Figure 21

Figure 23

Pattern 5 Figs 24, 25 and 26

12 pairs, 120/2 linen thread

To begin Hang two pairs round pin A and work the footside with two untwisted passive pairs; introduce two more pairs for the plait before putting up pin B and returning to the footside. Hang pairs round

pins and make a four-plait crossing at pin D. Plait to E and with picots to leaf M. From B plait introducing two new pairs at pin C; make a crossing at E with the plait from D.

Footside Two cloth passive pairs remain throughout; frequently the footside weaver absorbs and discards plait pairs (for example between F and G). On the curve below the flower pin, X is used twice.

Flower Leaves N, M and P meet at the six-plait crossing. The right-hand four threads make leaf Q which is taken into the footside and becomes additional passive pairs. The footside is worked and pairs released to work leaf R. The centre pin is removed and pairs remaining in the centre and those from R work another six-plait crossing. Leaves U, T and S complete the flower.

Figure 24

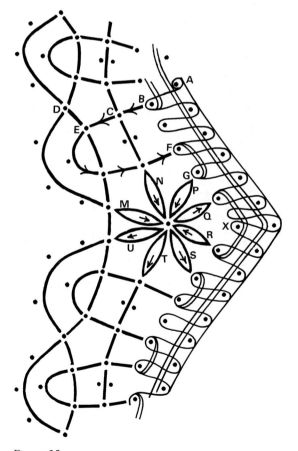

Figure 25

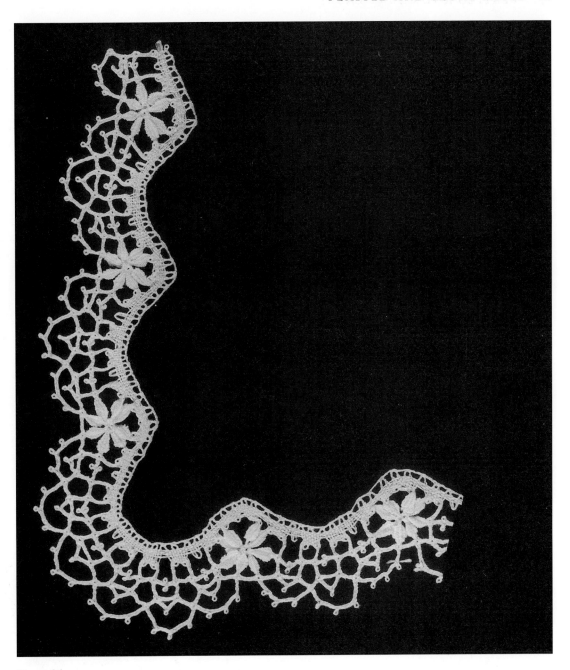

Figure 26

Pattern 6A Figs 27a and b, 28a and 29a

14 pairs, 100/2 linen thread

Hang four pairs round pin A. Twist the two threads on the extreme left three times and the two threads immediately left of the pin twice. Work cloth stitch and two twists with the pairs to the right of the pin; give the outer (right) pair one extra twist. Fig. 27b will clarify this. The inner pairs are the weavers for the footside; one will work down the right-hand side and the other around the curve and down the left-hand side. Allow the left pair to fall to the back of the pillow and place pins between the threads and heads of the bobbins to hold the pairs firmly.

Hang four pairs – to become the passives in both directions – around pin x and, using the weaver to the left of pin A, work in cloth stitch through the four threads to the right of pin x. Now work through the same passive pairs with the weaver to the right of pin A. Twist this weaver twice, put in pin S and return to work footside pin T. Continue to y.

Turn the pillow round, remove pin x and put in pin B between weaver and passive pairs. Work to the footside at pin C. Remove the pins steadying the outer pair. Work the footside stitch and continue to x where two pairs are added for the leaf. Similarly pairs are added at z.

Leaves are made from x, y and z and a six-plait crossing is worked in the centre. The illustration shows the arrangement of plaits and leaves.

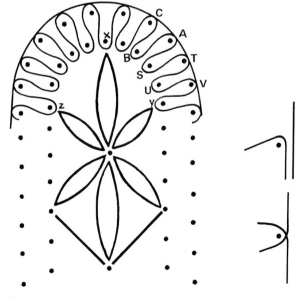

Figure 27a

Figure 27b

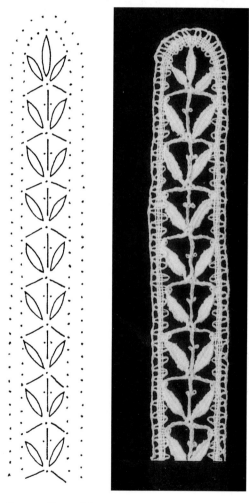

Figures 28a and 29a

Pattern 6B Figs 28b and 29b

This is worked similarly; leaves and plaits are arranged at the discretion of the lacemaker.

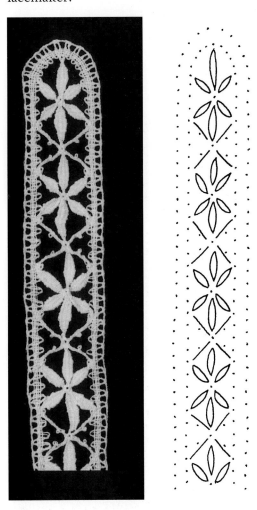

Figures 28b and 29b

Insertions

Lace with a footside on both sides may be used as the traditional insertion; but placed on coloured neckbands and cuffs it looks very attractive. Made with a pointed or rounded end the lace will become a centre strip for an easily made jabot. Refer to page 62.

Cluny patterns

Patterns 7, 8, 9 and 10 are often called
Cluny patterns although they were worked
in the East Midlands at the beginning of the
twentieth century. Scallops on the headside
and twists within the trails are characteristic
of this lace, so named as it is similar to lace
in the Cluny Museum in Paris.

Pattern 7   Figs 30, 31 and 32

12 pairs, 120/2 linen thread

Cloth stitch diamond Hang one pair on pin
a and two pairs side by side on each of pins
b, *c* and *d*. Begin using pairs from *a* and *b*,
work cloth stitch, twist the left-hand pair
twice and cover pin S with cloth stitch.
Remove pin *a* and pull the weaver thread
into position. Place another pair on pin *a*
and work the diamond taking in one pair at
each pin, and leaving out similarly until the
weaver and last pair work pin Z which is
covered with cloth stitch. Remove pins *a*, *b*,
c and *d*.

Footside Hang two pairs round pin A, twist
each three times and cover with cloth stitch
and two twists. Work in cloth stitch
through two passive pairs hung from pin *b*
and on through two pairs plaited from T/V.
Put in pin B and continue the footside to C,
D, E and G.

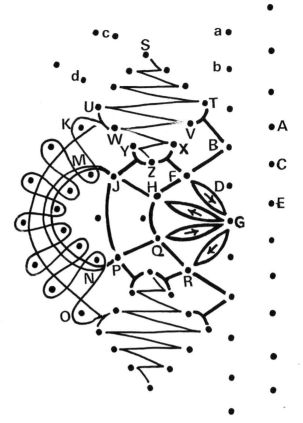

Figure 30

Leaves, plaits and headside Plaits from X/Z and from B cross at F. The right pairs from F make a leaf to G. The weaver works through them and pin G is put up. A leaf is made to H and a crossing made with a plait from F. Plaits from Y/Z and H cross at J. Pin K is put between plait pairs from U/W. Twist the left pair which becomes weaver and works cloth stitch and twist through the right pair, and cloth stitch through the plaited pairs from J. Pin M is put to the left of the weaver.

The scalloped headside is worked (two pairs in cloth stitch and the outer pair with cloth stitch and twist) to N and O. Remember, when weaving out to the left, to twist the weaver before working cloth and twist with the edge pair. From N, plait the pairs to P and work a crossing with the plait from J. Continue with a crossing at Q and a leaf to G. Remove pin G. Weave through the leaf pairs and replace pin G. Continue the footside. Make a leaf from G and plait from Q to cross at R. Plaits are made from O, P, R and the footside to begin the cloth stitch diamond.

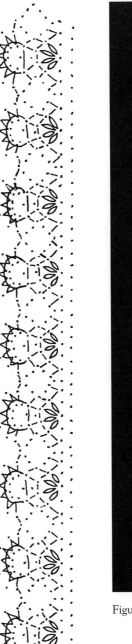

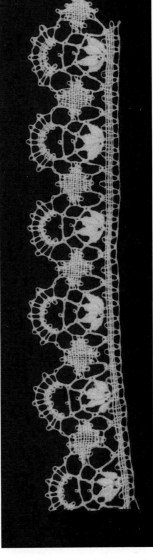

Figure 32

Figure 31

Pattern 8 Figs 33, 34 and 35

12 pairs, 120/2 linen thread

This pattern is similar to Pattern 7 but the cloth diamond is replaced by a triangle with twisted passives in the centre.

Footside Hang two pairs round pin A and work the footside through two passive pairs with cloth stitch to pin E.

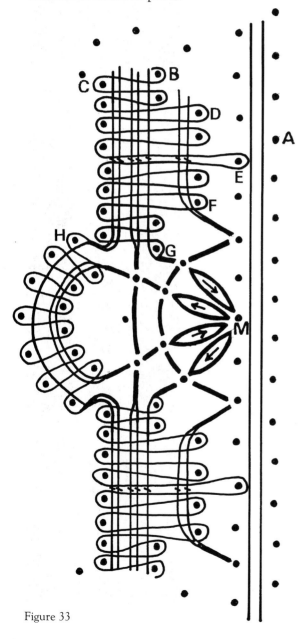

Figure 33

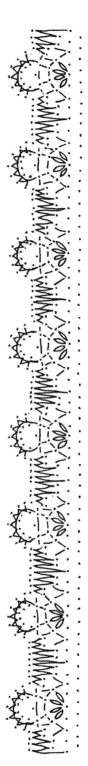

Figure 34

Cloth triangle Hang one weaver pair on pin B and weave in cloth stitch through four passive pairs, twist the weaver once and work through one pair more in cloth stitch and twist. Put up pin C. Twist the weaver and continue maintaining a cloth stitch and twist pair on the headside. Introduce two new pairs before pin D. The triangle weaver works cloth stitch, pin, cloth stitch with the footside weaver at E. Twist the triangle

passive pairs once. Continue working, leave out two pairs after pin F and stop at pin G. Headside pairs plait to H; the pin is put between the pairs and the outer pair becomes the weaver for the scallop.

Leaves and headside This is worked in the same way as the previous pattern. Pin M is used twice.

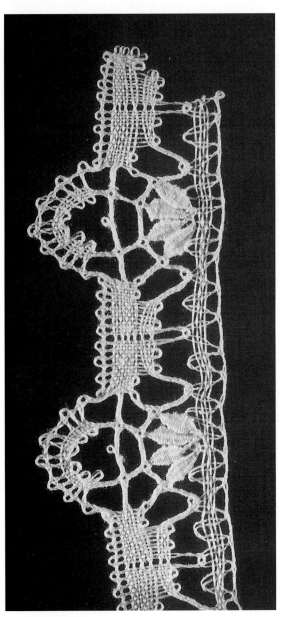

Figure 35 (detail)

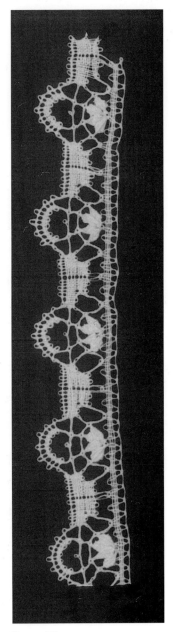

Figure 35

Pattern 9 Figs 36, 37 and 38

12 pairs, 120/2 linen thread

The working is similar to the previous patterns. Work the footside from A through two passive pairs and introduce two plait pairs at B. Continue to H. Hang pairs behind the work to make a six-plait crossing at C. Plait to E, J and H, work the footside and continue to K. Place two pairs round D and cover with cloth stitch and twist. With cloth stitch bring in the plait pairs at E; continue to G. Plait pairs from F and make a six-plait crossing at J. Make plaits to N and K. Continue the footside to B1.

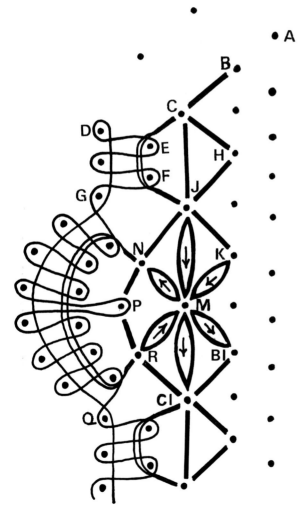

Figure 37

Figure 36

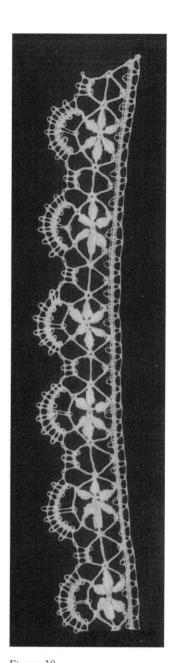

Figure 38

Leaves from K and J make a four-plait
crossing at M and the left pairs make
another leaf to N. Make the crossing and
the scalloped headside from G. Before P the
weaver is twisted and works cloth stitch
through the plait pairs from N. The head is
continued in the usual way to Q. Pairs from
the scallop plait back for the crossing at R
and then make the leaf to the centre.
Remove pin M and make a four-plait
crossing with the leaf pairs and the hanging
pairs, using hole M a second time. Make
leaves to B1 and C1.

NOTE C and J are six-plait crossings but M
has two four-plait crossings.

Pricking 39 for a small circular mat is
worked similarly.

Figure 39

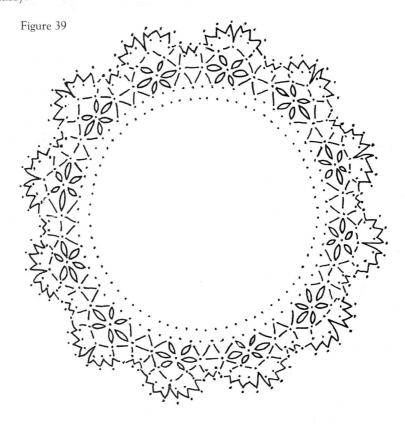

Pattern 10 Figs 40, 41 and 42

The working is similar to Pattern 9. Refer
to instructions for introducing pairs on
page 36.

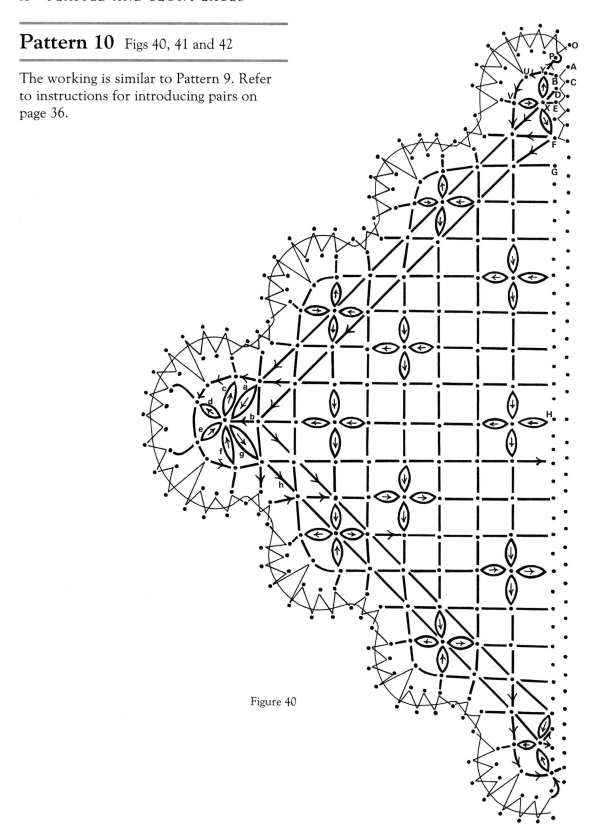

Figure 40

Figure 41

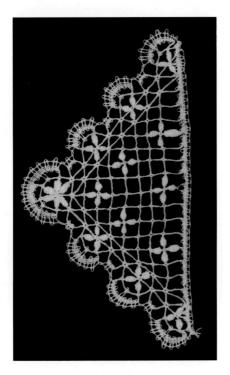

To begin Hang eight pairs round pin A. The two threads to the right of the pin weave in cloth stitch to the left through four pairs. Twist the weaver and last pair once, put up pin O; cover with cloth stitch and twist.

Return to pin A and weave with the right-hand two threads through all pairs (five), put up pin B and return through four pairs in cloth stitch. Twist the weaver twice and the remaining pair three times, work the footside pin C. The left side pairs are plaited to Y and the other two are footside passives.

Continue the footside to join in plait pairs at D and E. These make a four-plait crossing at X. Left-hand pairs make a leaf and work a crossing at Y. The left-hand pairs plait to P and become passives in the scalloped headside. The right-hand pairs are plaited to U and V. The scallop passives are plaited for the crossing at V and make a leaf to X. Another four-plait crossing is made and pin replaced. At F the leaf pairs are linked in and two pairs are added for the other plait. Plait pairs are added on the footside as required as far as H. After H plait pairs are discarded in the footside. Refer to page 37.

Centre flower Leaf *a* and the plait from *b* make a crossing; leaves *c* and *d* are made. These return as leaves *e* and *f*, and the threads of one pair from *e* is hooked under between *c* and *a* and the other pair passes through the loop. This ensures that the four-plait crossing which is now worked with *e* and *f* is linked into the flower centre. Two threads are discarded and darned into leaves *e* and *f*, the remaining six make leaf *g*. For this leaf, the leaf weaver and centre thread are single threads, but the edge threads are double. Continue into plait *h* and discard two threads. The selection of threads is important and the choice for each position is more easily seen on the pillow.

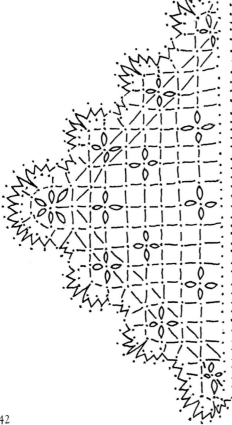

Figure 42

2

Introductory edgings and insertions

Techniques

By studying a pricking and when possible referring to lace or a photograph, it is possible to work out where to start and how many pairs to use. If misjudged, pairs can be added or discarded as explained on page 36. It is unnecessary to undo and restart the lace.

To begin a pattern

The lacemaker has to learn to select a suitable position. When inexperienced, select that part of the lace where the position of pairs is obvious and easily understood. If the lace has to be joined, it is important to consider how this will be achieved. It is easier to sew into a cloth area than join into plait crossings. Traditionally the lace was overlapped by one complete repeat and the ends hidden inside. This ensured that the finished article would withstand laundering and use. If the lace is gathered this method shows very little.

Headside

The headside, on the left side of the lace, may be finished in a variety of ways – undecorated cloth, cloth with picots or an arrangement of plaits. The last is particularly typical of Bedfordshire lace.

Ninepin Fig. 43*a*. This has been explained on page 18.

Fig. 43*b*. This method is frequently found in old lace. The pairs from the plait remain in the trail for two pins and therefore increase the width of the trail which appears uneven. Many people adapt a pattern so that the ninepin can be worked as Fig 43*a*, which may be easier to work but sadly changes the appearance of the lace.

Fig. 43*c*. Occasionally, to avoid thickening the trail more than is absolutely necessary, a single pair may be used as shown. It is twisted from the trail to *r*, works cloth stitch through the plait pairs; pin *r* is put up and the weaver twisted before working back through the plait pairs. It is twisted to *s*, pin *s* is worked as pin *r* and it is twisted back to the footside.

Fig. 43*d*. The use of leaves adds decoration; refer to page 11.

Double ninepin A more complicated form of decorative plaiting. There are many variations.

Fig. 44*a*. A simple form which does not hold its shape.

Fig. 44*b*. Plaits cross with a four-plait crossing at *a*.

Fig. 44*c*. Before picots *t* and *u* are made the inner pairs of plaits cross with cloth stitch and twist. Similarly the plaits are linked before picots *w* and *v* are made.

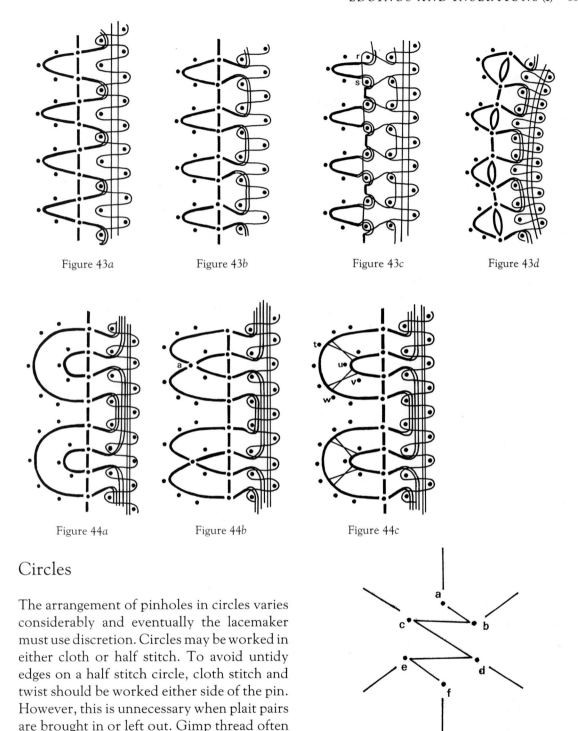

Figure 43a   Figure 43b   Figure 43c   Figure 43d

Figure 44a   Figure 44b   Figure 44c

Circles

The arrangement of pinholes in circles varies considerably and eventually the lacemaker must use discretion. Circles may be worked in either cloth or half stitch. To avoid untidy edges on a half stitch circle, cloth stitch and twist should be worked either side of the pin. However, this is unnecessary when plait pairs are brought in or left out. Gimp thread often encircles half stitch. Pairs should be twisted twice either side of the gimp thread.

Fig. 45a. Pin a is put between the plait pairs and covered. Two pairs are brought in at each of pins b and c and left out after pins d and e.

Figure 45a

The weaver works through the final centre pair, pin f is put up and covered in preparation for the plait or leaf.

Fig. 45b. Pairs are used as described for Fig. a. At u and v it is usual to link with other features. Alternatively, one pair from each plait is brought in at b and c and the other pairs at v and u. Pairs are left out similarly.

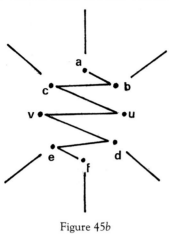

Figure 45b

Holes within cloth stitch circles

Six-pin hole Fig. 46a. Work normally and stop at o when the weaver and centre pair have worked a cloth stitch. Put up pin o and cover with cloth stitch. Both pairs act as weavers as shown in the diagram. These meet at p; work a cloth stitch, pin p is put up and covered with cloth stitch. One pair becomes a passive and the other weaves to complete the circle.

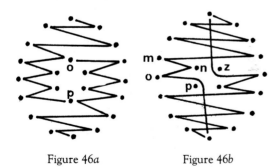

Figure 46a   Figure 46b

Four-pin hole Fig. 46b. The weaver works to m, n, o and is supported by pin p. The centre pair is supported by pin z and becomes the weaver for the remaining cloth stitch.

Figure 46c

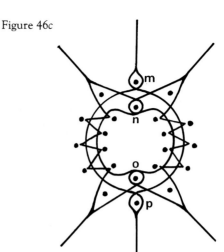

The hole within a cloth ring Fig. 46c. Pairs at m provide the outside passive pairs. The inner plait pairs become the inner passives at n, and the other plait pairs become the weavers for each side of the circle. The inner passives from o and the weavers form the side plaits and the centre plait is formed by pairs from p.

Trails

The trail provides a convenient means of carrying threads from one part of the pattern to another, also it provides a place to discard unwanted pairs. It is worked in cloth stitch, the weaver twisted two or three times as it passes round the pin.

Adding/Discarding pairs

Pairs for leaves/plaits Fig. 47a. Hang two pairs round a pin and work cloth stitch through the threads to one side of the pin. Continue the cloth stitch trail and remove the pin, pull the pairs down and use as required.

NOTE Fig. 47b. When beginning a piece of lace it is often necessary to add pairs into the trail as if from a plait or leaf. Hang pairs

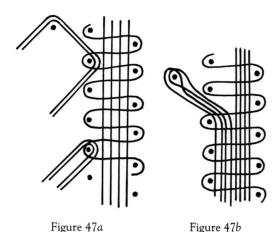

Figure 47a   Figure 47b

side by side on a support pin and take the
weaver through them normally.

**One pair to increase the trail passives
(Method 1)** Fig. 48a. Work to the edge of
the trail, twist the weaver and hold firmly.
Take one pair under the weaver and behind
the pin and allow the threads to fall inside
one thread. Continue.

**One pair to increase the trail passives
(Method 2)** Fig. 48b. Work to the edge of
the trail. Allow two threads from a support
pin to fall in position as shown. Continue
to work the trail. Eventually the ends will
be cut close to the trail. It is important to
ensure these threads remain in the trail and
are not used for a plait until established.

To reduce the number of pairs in the trail
Fig. 49. Work to the edge of the trail.
Remove a pair as shown, avoid adjacent
threads. The threads are laid back so that
the bobbins hang to the back of the pillow.
Again it is necessary to ensure that the
threads to be discarded are established;
never throw out pairs recently added. Pairs
will be cut off close to the trail later.

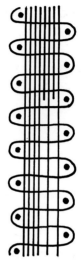

Figure 49

**Taking pairs in from/out for plaits or
leaves** The recognized traditional method is
shown in Fig. 50a. The presence of one or
two pairs gives the appearance of continuity
when there is rapid change-over of trail
pairs. However, when plaits are
conveniently placed or it would enhance the
design to achieve a trail with the same
passive pairs, plait pairs may be taken
directly through the trail. This is shown in

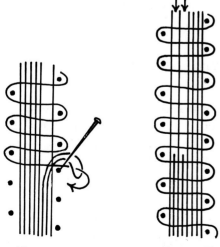

Figure 48a   Figure 48b

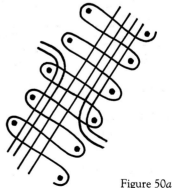

Figure 50a

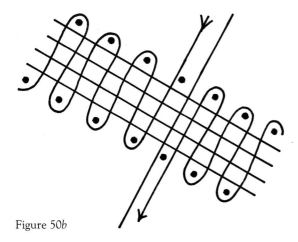

Figure 50b

Fig. 50b. The weaver is left out to become part of the plait, the first pair from the plait entering the trail travels directly across, these make the new plait and the second pair becomes the new weaver. This method should be used with caution as it may detract from the traditional appearance.

Linking trails

Fig. 51a. The weaver from each trail works cloth stitch and two twists, pin, cloth stitch to cover the pin and continue. In this way there are no twists in the trail but only round the pin within the stitches.

Fig. 51b. The pins are put up in each trail and the weavers – twisted two or three times according to the space – work together with cloth stitch and two or three twists. They continue, working the other trail.

Fig. 51c. The weavers work a tally as described on page 11.

Curved or pointed trails

Fig 52a. A trail worked normally.

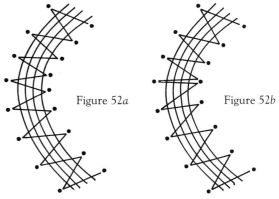

Figure 52a   Figure 52b

Fig 52b. The centre hole is used twice. On the second occasion the pin is removed, the lace pushed back and the hole re-used. There is only one weaver pair around the pin as work proceeds.

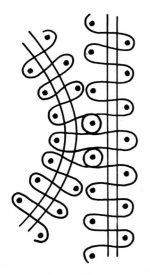

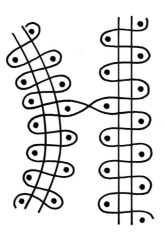

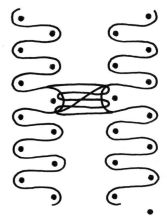

Figure 51a   Figure 51b   Figure 51c

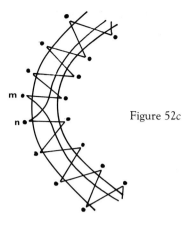

Figure 52c

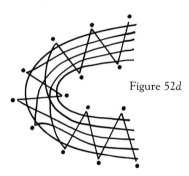

Figure 52d

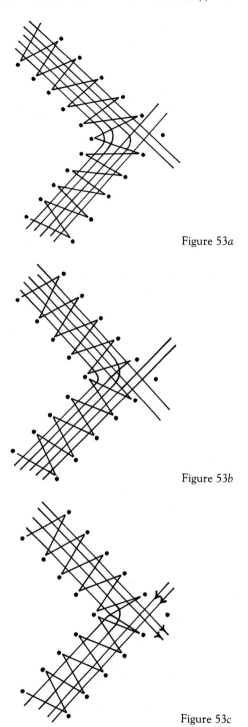

Figure 53a

Figure 53b

Figure 53c

Fig 52c. From pin *m* take the weaver through some of the passive pairs and allow it to become a passive. Take another pair to pin *n* as the new weaver. The position in which the original weaver lies depends on the shape and thickness of the trail.

Fig. 52d. Similar to Fig. 52c but repetition may be necessary to accommodate the number of holes on the outer edge.

Fig. 53a, b and c. Between the heads plait pairs can be brought directly into the trail and exchanged for other trail pairs without the use of the weaver. The use of edge and third pair helps to prevent a hole appearing in the trail. This method may be combined with the exchange of weavers shown in Fig. 53b. As shown in Fig. 53c it is not always necessary to alternate the pairs taken for the plait.

When the plaits travel to and from an inner trail, refer to Fig. 151 (centre) on page 100; square leaves are sometimes made instead of plaits. This can give the illusion of crossing trails and improves the appearance of the lace.

Pattern 11 Figs. 54, 55 and 56

D.M.C. Broder Machine no. 50

To calculate the number of pairs required

In previous patterns instructions have included the number of pairs used when setting up. However, the requirement may vary according to the thickness of thread and/ or the tension of the worker, particularly when working trails or areas of cloth or half stitch. The pattern should look attractive and, to achieve this, an experienced lacemaker will add pairs as required.

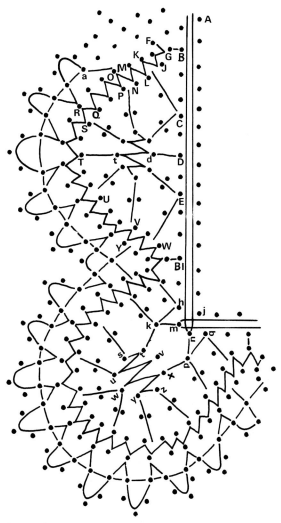

Figure 54

To assess the number of pairs required for pattern 11

At footside, four pairs – two for the edge and two passive pairs.

At T a weaver and several (three?) passive pairs.

At J, N and Q two pairs for each plait.

Ninepin edge, four pairs for two plaits.

Approximately 18 pairs are required.

Footside and trail Work the footside from A. Begin the trail with a weaver on pin F. Hang seven pairs on a support pin and weave to G. Put up pins G and B, twist the weavers twice and work cloth stitch and twist. They continue in opposite trails. Continue the trail. Two pairs are left out after pin J – therefore from K to L the weaver travels through five pairs only. Two new pairs, to become part of the trail, are introduced at M (refer to Fig. 47*b*). Two pairs are introduced for a plait at O (refer to Fig. 47*a*). Pairs are left out after pin N (the weaver from O to P will travel through seven pairs – five trail and two ninepin pairs) and after pin Q the weaver from R to S will travel through five pairs – three trail pairs and two ninepin pairs. Continue the trail to T.

Ninepin edge Introduce two pairs at the crossing *a*. Ninepin instructions are given in Pattern 3 on page 18. The arrangement of plaits between the heads is shown in the diagram.

Footside Continue the footside to D linking in a plait at C.

Half stitch circle Refer to Fig 45*b*. Make plaits and picots from C, N and Q. To achieve a tidy circle, work cloth and twist with the weaver and edge pair at *d*. The weavers from *d* and D are twisted three times and work cloth stitch and twist and continue in the new position. T is worked similarly.

To complete one repeat

Make plaits from the circle to E, U, V and W.
Work the footside to B1, linking in the plait at
E. Work the ninepin and trail bringing in
pairs at U, V and W. Leave out two pairs after
pin Y.

The corner Four additional pairs are
necessary to work the two extra plaits. They
are added according to Figs 47*a* or 48*b*. The
former is the easier method. Fig. 49 explains
the method for removing the pairs – use of
the same method for introduction and
removal will give a balanced trail on the
corner curve.

Footside Link in the plait at *h* and complete
corner pin *j*. Make the crossing *k* and put
pin *m* between the plait pairs. These work
cloth stitch through the footside passives
and replace them. The old passives lie either
side of pin *n* and are plaited to *p*.

Half-stitch circle Work from *s* through to
cloth stitch and twist pin *v* cloth stitch and
twist. At *w* the plait pairs are linked using
cloth stitch.

To complete the corner Make the crossing
at *p*. The corner footside weaver continues
linking in the plait at *q*. Complete the trail;
leave out the four pairs added for plaits.

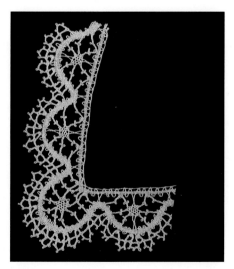

Figure 55

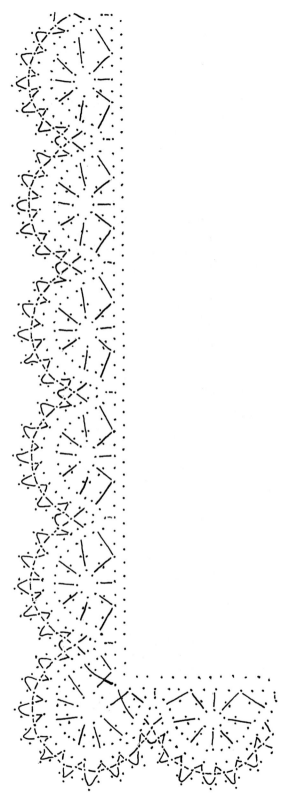

Figure 56

Pattern 12 Figs 57 and 58

D.M.C. Broder Machine no. 50

This is similar to the previous pattern.
Leaves are worked from N to the half-stitch
circle and then to V. The pricking shows
clearly the arrangement of plaits and picots
on the headside.

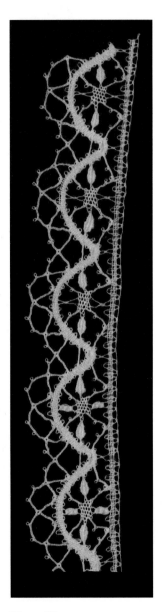

Figure 57

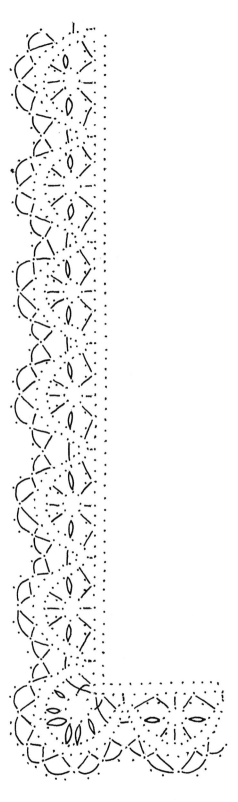

Figure 58

Pattern 13 Figs 59, 60 and 61

D.M.C. Broder Machine no. 50

To begin the footside Use the method explained in Figs 27a and b. Introduce ten pairs into the trail; this will provide five passive pairs in each direction. Two will be required for the footside, two for the inner trail and one for inner trail weaver. Pairs for plaits and the leaf are joined in at a, b and c. The weaver from r works through three passive pairs; put in pin s and cover. Both pairs become weavers with two pairs in each trail. Work t and u similarly.

The circle is worked in half stitch; tallies are made at e and f.

The trails are linked at positions g, h and j on both sides with cloth stitch and twist. The weavers from q and r work through two cloth pairs, are twisted once and work through one leaf pair and then together with cloth stitch. Put up pin s, cover with cloth stitch and work back to t and u, twisting between plait and trail pairs. At v and w the trail and footside weavers work together with cloth stitch, pin, cloth stitch.

To work the insertion without the shape end, begin at V, W, q and r.

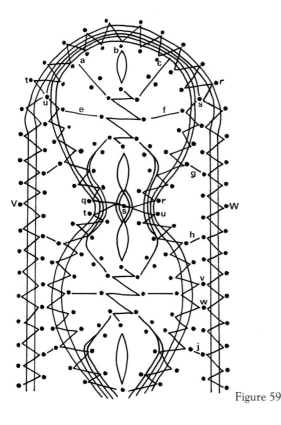

Figure 59

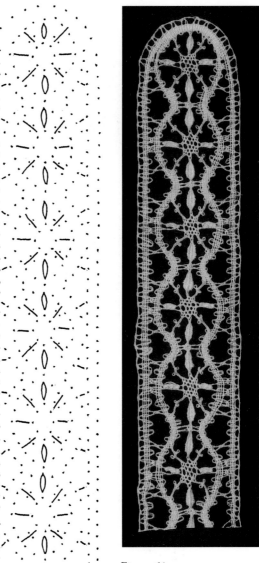

Figure 61

Figure 60

Pattern 14 Figs 62, 63 and 64

100/2 linen thread

Known as the feather pattern, this was one of the Winslow (a Buckinghamshire village) Industry patterns.

The trail Hang a weaver on K and work through four passive pairs to L. Add two pairs at M for the leaf. Leave out one pair at each pin n, o, p, q, r and s. Introduce a new pair at each pin O, P, Q, R and S. From pin S twist the outer passive pair. Twist the weaver before the edge pair and work cloth stitch and twist pin T, cloth stitch and twist. This edge will be worked until pairs are left out from U. Twist the pair from n three times, o, p and q twice and from r and s once. The weaver from u works cloth stitch and twist through all pairs to d. Give the weaver pair one twist extra between each stitch.

The footside Begin at pin A and introduce five passive pairs – the arrangement is discretionary – and work to B.

The circle Work the half stitch circle introducing two pairs at a, two at b and those from the leaf from M. The weavers work together with cloth stitch and twist at d and at c/B. Continue, follow the diagram.

The corner: Footside The diagram is self-explanatory. Work in letter order. The footside weaver passes round pin C without working the edge stitch and continues to D. After the inner passive has passed round pin J it returns to corner pin C when the edge stitch is worked. Pins e, g and h merely support pairs to maintain a square corner.

Trail Two pairs are required for a plait to v, also pairs are added singly as far as w. The appearance will be improved if pairs are added each time the weaver travels inward from u, refer to Fig. 48b. From x, pairs are discarded.

Centre The half stitch weaver at y works a tally with the left-side pair at the crossing z.

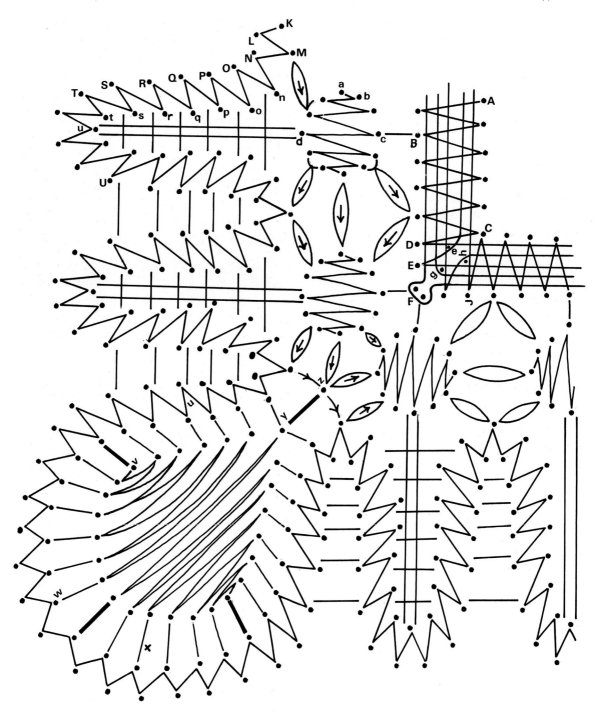

Figure 62

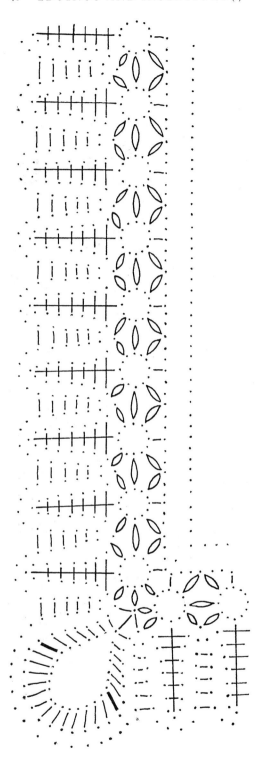

Figure 63

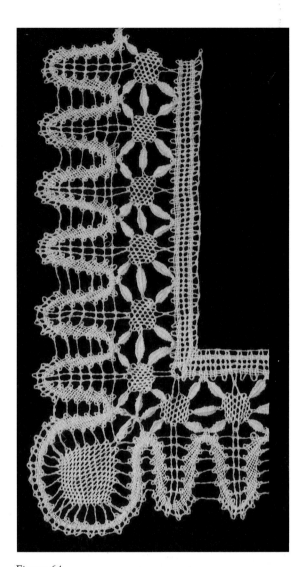

Figure 64

Pattern 15   Figs 65, 66 and 67

D.M.C. Broder Machine no. 50

The method of beginning with a curved footside has been explained on page 24. Add two pairs at *a* for a plait as described in Fig. 47*a*. Similarly join in four pairs at *b*. Again in the same way join in four pairs at *c*. The left-hand threads become part of the cloth trail; the right-hand threads make a plait. Put pin *d* between the plait pairs from *s*. These become trail passive pairs. Cross the weavers with cloth stitch and twist at *e*. The weaver at *f* travels through four pairs from the leaves and back to the footside. The method for taking plait pairs through the trail for use on the other side is explained in Fig. 50*b*. For use as an insertion the pattern should be started with three trails from footside pins A and C and inner trail pin B. Pairs are also added at crossing D.

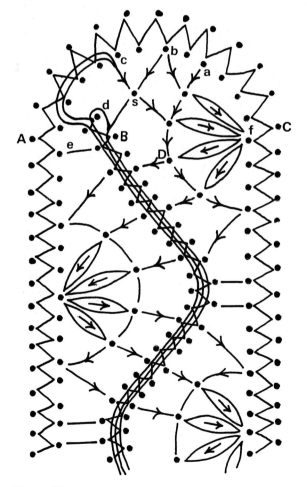

Figure 65

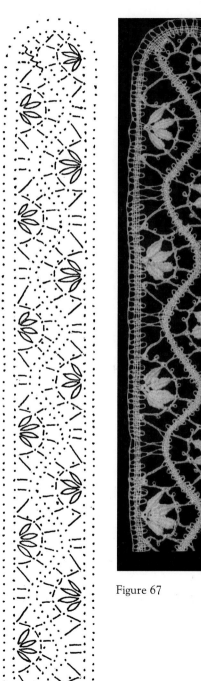

Figure 66

Figure 67

Pattern 16 Figs 68, 69a and b, 70

Broder Machine no. 30

The pattern is straightforward to work although attention is needed to achieve a flat and neat point at *f*.

To begin Set in the footside from A and hang in two pairs for a plait at B. Hang a weaver on *a* and work through eight pairs in cloth stitch. Continue the trail leaving out two pairs at pin *c*. Work to *d*. Plait from *c* and join in two pairs at the four-plait crossing at *x*. Plait pairs to *y* and *z*. Hang up two more pairs for the crossing at *y*.

The trail Follow detailed Diagrams 69a and *b*. At *f* two pairs work through each other in cloth stitch; this is not a four-plait crossing. Six-plait crossings are worked at *p* and *r* and a four-plait crossing at *q*.

The corner Six extra pairs will be needed for the plaits. Refer to the diagram and work the crossings in order *j*, *k*, *l*, *m*, *n* and *o*. Discard the six unwanted pairs in the trail.

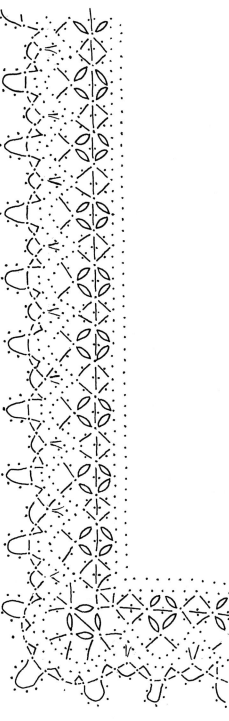

Figure 68

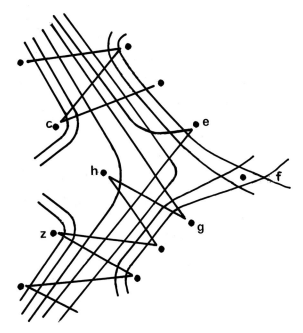

Figure 69*b*

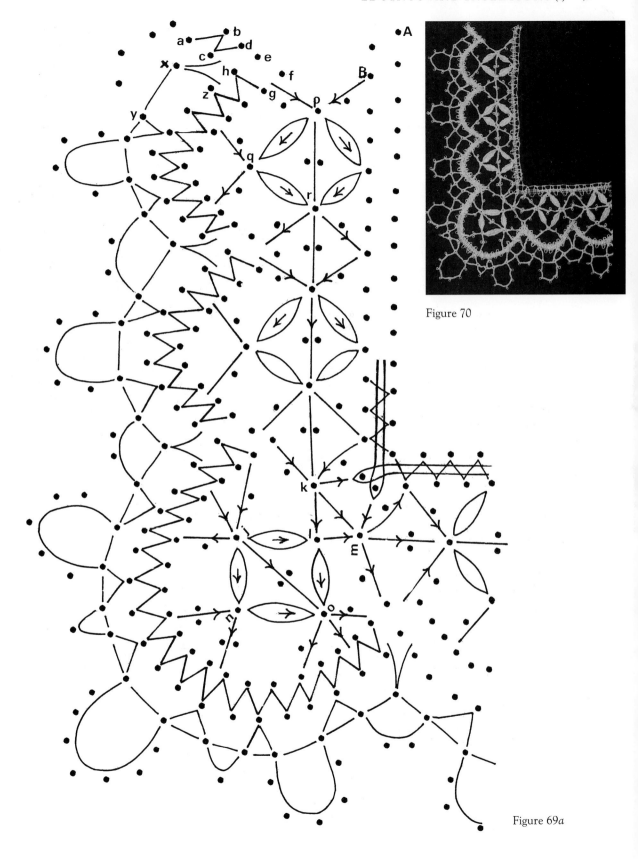

Figure 70

Figure 69a

Pattern 17 Figs 71, 72 and 73

120/2 linen thread

For raised tallies refer to Fig. 8 on page 12.
Begin as described for pattern 6A on page
24. Add pairs for plaits at *a*, *b*, *c*, *d* and *e*.
To work as an insertion hang up pairs for
four-plait crossings at *n* and *m*. Set up the
footsides from *p* and *q*. Two pairs are also
required at pin *r*.

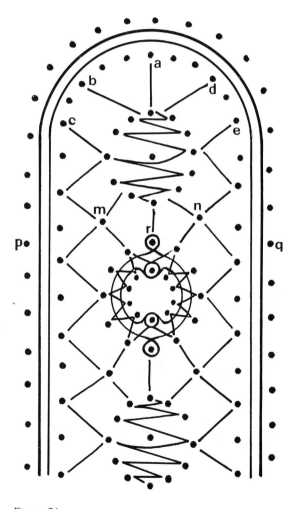

Figure 71

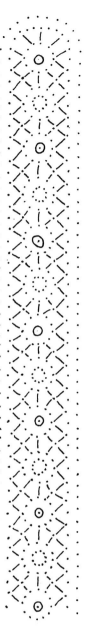

Figure 72

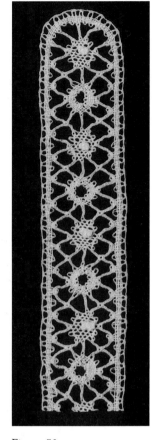

Figure 73

Pattern 18 Figs 74, 75 and 76

120/2 linen thread

This pattern has a particularly interesting combination of techniques. Square leaves

create the illusion of crossing trails. Plait pairs travel through the trails by the Cluny method (page 38) to avoid unnecessary thickness. Elsewhere pairs are taken in to become part of the trail and left out when required for another feature.

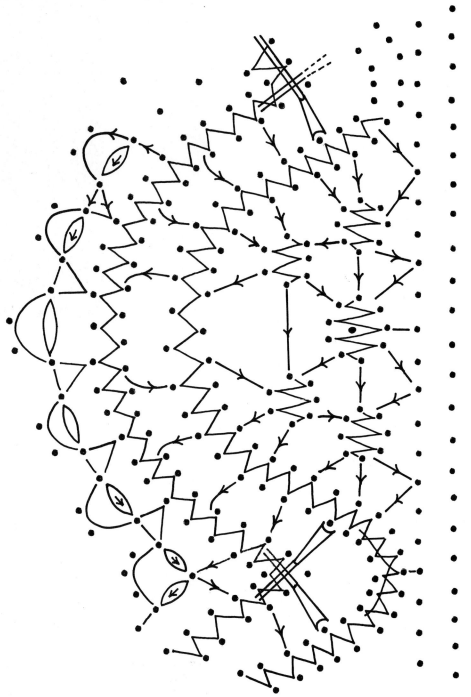

Figure 74

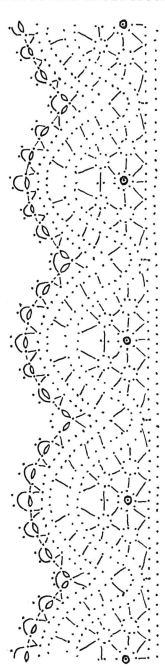

Figure 75

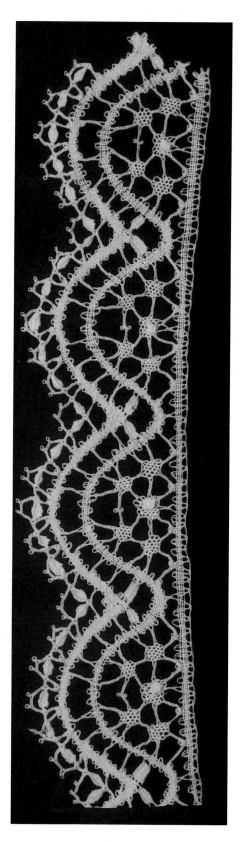

Figure 76

Pattern 19 Figs 77, 78 and 79

120/2 linen thread

Work the oval half stitch feature introducing two pairs each at a, b and c. Hang a weaver round pin H and introduce nine pairs, three to maintain the trail and six for plaits from d, e and f. The trail weaver works cloth and twist with the oval

bud weaver at g. Cloth stitch and twist either side of the pin is required for a firm result at h. Hang pairs round pin A and set in the footside. Join in two pairs for the plait from B.

The half stitch circle weaver works cloth stitch and twist at pins k and m.

Two extra pairs are needed in the corner trail for the plait n; they are discarded after o.

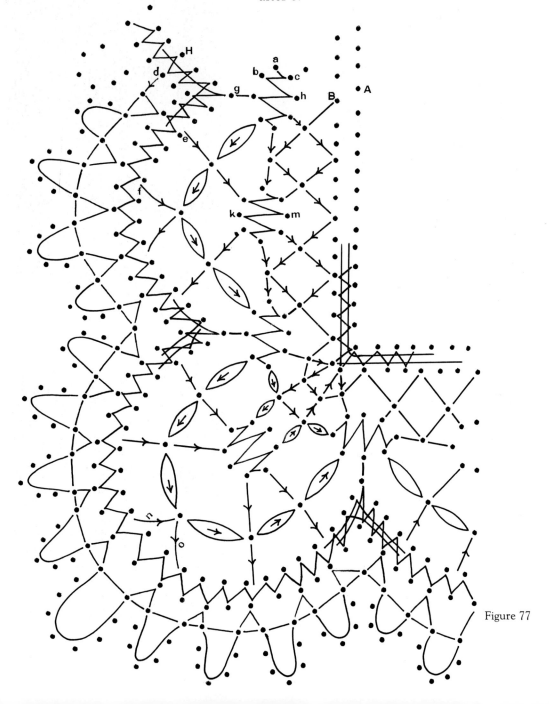

Figure 77

Figure 79

Figure 78

Pattern 20   Figs 80, 81 and 82

Work the footside from A to *b* as usual and continue to *c* and join in two plait pairs. Hang a weaver pair on *d* and work through eight pairs to *e* to begin the trail. Pairs from *f* and the vertical plait begin the circle and the other plaits are joined in at *n* and *o*.

To maintain a good edge it is essential to use cloth stitch and twist at the other pins.

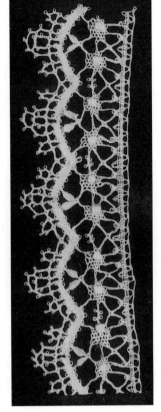

Figure 81

Figure 82

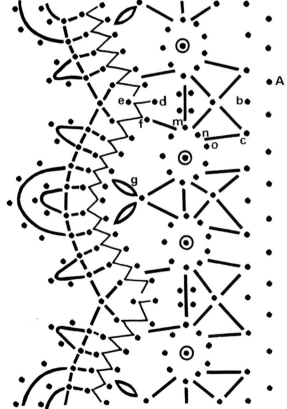

Figure 80

3

Edgings and insertions

Trails: crossed; joined; branching

The beauty of many Bedfordshire designs lies in the flowing nature of the trails. Before working the pattern it is important to appreciate the dominance of some trails and the temporary importance of others. This can be expressed sympathetically in the lace and will help the less experienced worker to interpret the pricking successfully.

Crossed trails

Fig. 83*a*. When all pairs cross (i.e. there is the same number of pairs in both trails) the weavers meet at *a* with cloth stitch, pin, cloth stitch, and work back to *b* and *c*. Cross the passive pairs through each other as shown. The weavers work through to meet again at *d* with cloth stitch, pin, cloth stitch and then continue the trails.

Fig. 83*b*. When there are more pairs on one side than the other, leave the extra pairs at the outside edge and cross the others as described above.

Fig. 83*c*. When a leaf or plait complicates the crossing, work according to the diagram. The weavers travel through one plait pair each, work the cloth stitch, the pin is covered and the weavers travel back to the outside. The leaf pairs may be crossed before becoming passive pairs for the crossing.

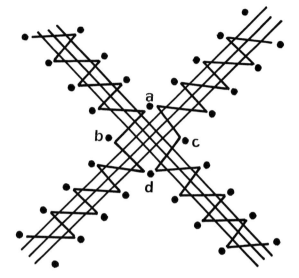

Figure 83*a*

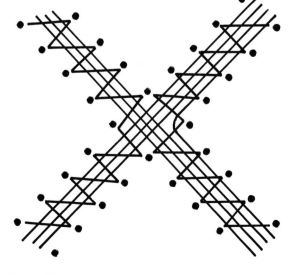

Figure 83*b*

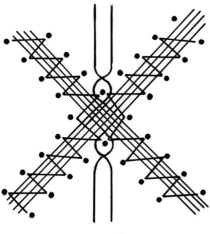

Figure 83c

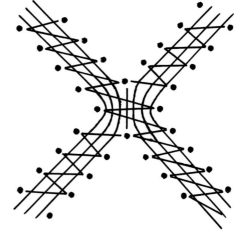

Figure 84b

Joined trails

Figs 84a, b and c. It was more common for the traditional lacemaker to retain one weaver which worked through both trails.

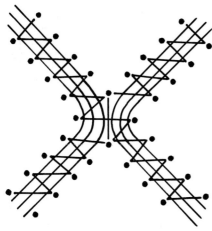

Figure 84a

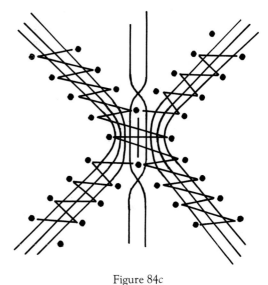

Figure 84c

Branching trails

Fig. 85a. The weavers join at the centre pin and one becomes a passive pair in the centre. If necessary, passive pairs can be discarded to avoid overcrowding the passives.

Fig. 85b. Similarly, a convenient passive will become a new weaver when two trails are developed from one.

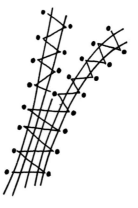

Figure 85a

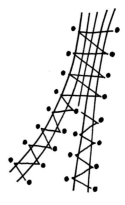

Figure 85b

Pattern 21 Figs 86, 87 and 88

Headside trail This requires a weaver, four pairs, one single thread and a gimp thread. The gimp thread lies on the outside edge and is used as an ordinary passive thread. The weaver makes a picot on the edge.

The inner trail This requires a weaver and three pairs of bobbins. Pairs from three plaits enter the inner trail, two pairs are left out for the flower centre, the others remain in the trail until required. When the trails run close together at *a*, twist the weavers and work cloth stitch and twist. The weavers change trails to continue.

The leaf centre Pairs are left out as shown in the diagram. Twist each pair three times and make square leaves to the centre putting pins between the leaf pairs. Twist pairs three times and cross the pairs as shown using cloth stitch and three twists. Make two leaves and twist all pairs three times.

It is usual for the weaver thread to cross the leaf and finish on the opposite side. Note the choice of weaver thread for each leaf – the second travelling to the right over the third or the third travelling to the left under the second. It is important to ensure that the centre pairs that make the first cloth stitch and three twists do not use the leaves' weavers. Refer to Fig. 158*a*.

The corner is formed from the inner trail and is continuous. The weaver takes in the outer trail weaver at *g*. Three pairs are left out at *h*, the outer trail pairs taken in at *j* and one pair for a weaver left out at *k*. Similarly the weaver is taken in at *m*, pairs are left out for the outer trail at *n*, pairs are taken in at *o* and a weaver left out at *p*.

The centre circle has a leaf over the half stitch. Work to *r*. Place the two centre pairs to the back, out of the working area. Work,

without these pairs, to *s*. Bring the pairs forward, twist twice and make a square leaf, twist pairs twice and place in position in the centre. Complete the circle including these pairs.

Figure 86

Figure 87

Figure 88

Pattern 22 Figs 89, 90 and 91

The crossing is similar to Fig. 83c. Weavers from q and r each work through one leaf pair before they meet at pin s. They travel to t and u. Three pairs from each side cross and the weavers meet at v. When continuing trails, leaf pairs are left out on either side of v.

For the working of the raised tally refer to Fig. 8. Tallies at f and g create the impression of a flower centre with eight petals (leaves).

To work the pattern as an insertion begin at M, N, O and P.

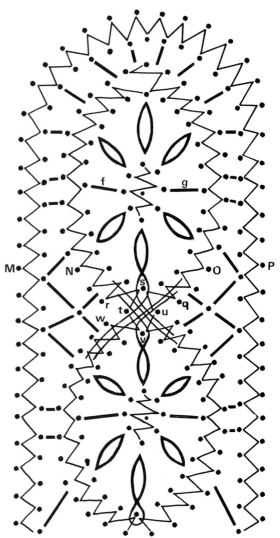

Figure 89

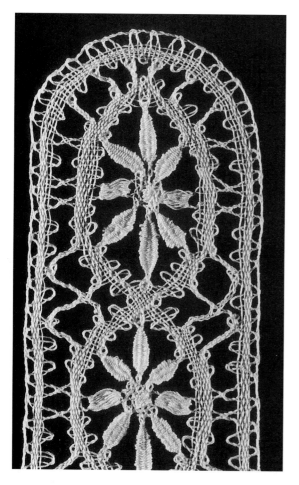

Figure 90 (detail)

Figure 90

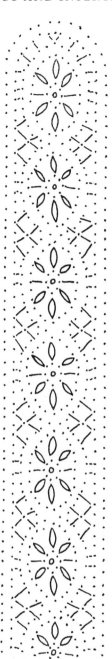

Figure 91

Pattern 23 Figs 92, 93 and 94

This pattern complements Pattern 22 and is very suitable to be gathered around it to make a jabot. A length of at least 30 in. (750 mm) is required.

Begin with four trails, the footside from A with two passive pairs, from *a* and *b* each with five passive pairs and from *c* with nine. Two pairs are required also at *d*, *e*, *f* and *g*. The crossing is worked as Pattern 22.

To make the jabot use three pins to mark the edging into four equal lengths. Pull up one passive thread to gather it into four equal sections; the total length must be the same as the edge of the centre insertion. Lay the edging to the wrong side of the insertion, overlapping the passive threads. Pin together and neatly sew along the footside insertion edge. The gathered edge is hidden underneath. The lace ends should be enclosed within a narrow binding.

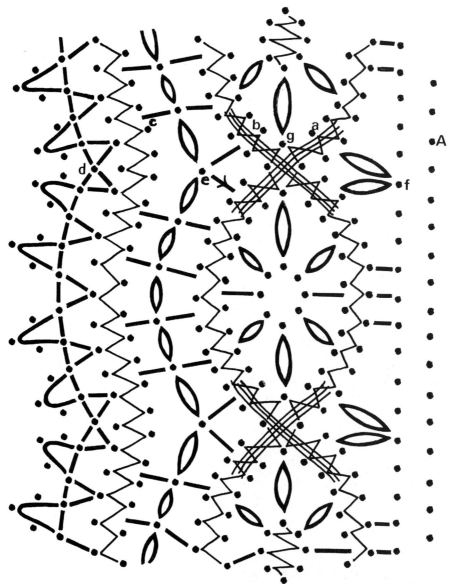

Figure 92

Figure 93

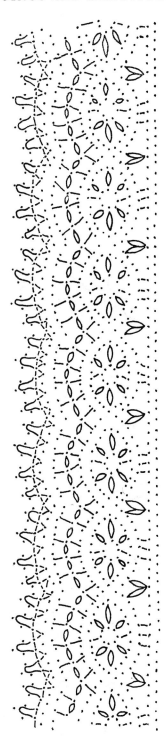

Figure 94

Pattern 24 Figs 95, 96 and 97

To begin hang two pairs round *a* and cover with cloth stitch. Hang four pairs on the left and three on the right. The crossing is worked as Fig. 83*b*. Two pairs are joined in at *x*, *y* and *z*.

Weavers meet to work tallies at *e/f* and *g/h*. As indicated by the difference in pricking and diagram, leaves or plaits may be worked in the ground.

The corner Pairs are added at *k* and *m* and twisted to *n* for a leaf. Two pairs are added at *o* for the leaf to *p*. It is joined into the trail at *q* and then pairs will be discarded. Two more pairs are discarded when the corner is complete, these were joined in for the leaf from *n*.

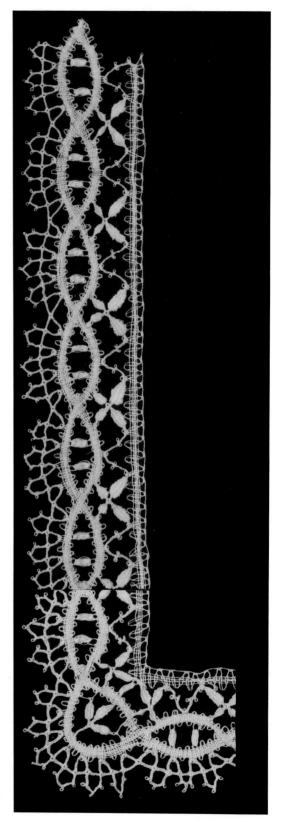

Figure 95

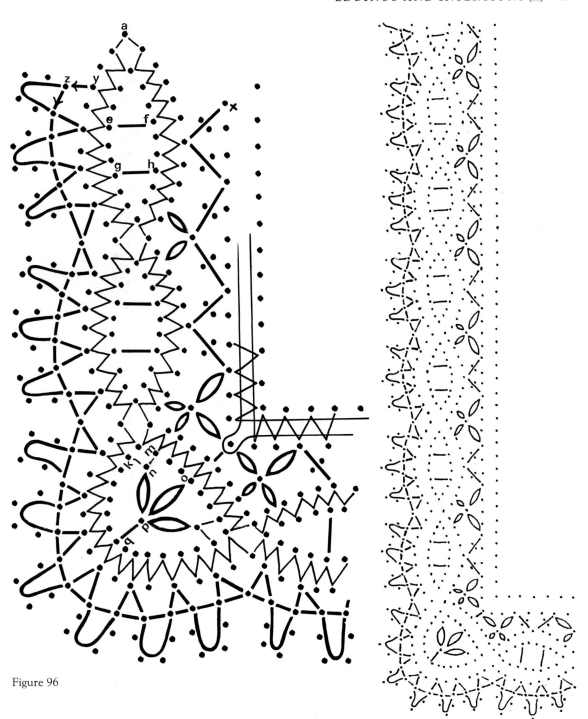

Figure 96

Figure 97

Pattern 25 Figs 98, 99 and 100

To begin hang two pairs round pin *a* and cover with cloth stitch, take these weavers to *b* and *c* through five passive pairs on each side. The crossing is worked as Fig. 83c. Pairs will be left out either side of *d* for a plait. One pair is added at *o* and two pairs at *p*.

The ring *k* is described in Fig. 46c. The footside is started at A. Therefore four support pins, each with two pairs, are required to work the ring.

To work the cloth block *m* a pin is put between the plait pairs and the left-hand pair works through the right-hand pair, the leaf pairs and the other plait pairs. At the end the pin is put to the left of the weaver and these pairs make the plait to the footside.

The small trail Two pairs are left out at *e* and one at *f*. The trail is worked to *o* where the weavers meet and the two passive pairs are joined in at *p*.

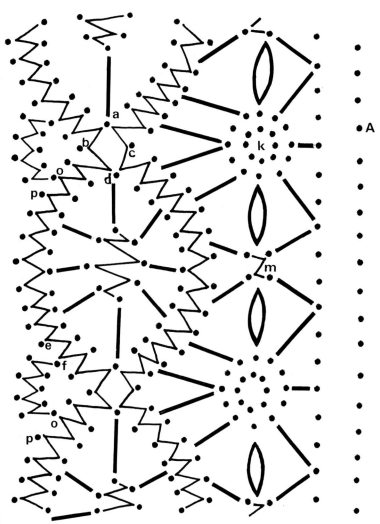

Figure 98

Figure 99

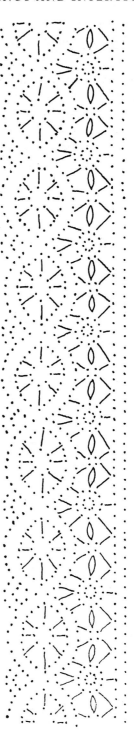

Figure 100

Pattern 26   Figs 101, 102 and 103

The footside and small trail At *m* the trail weaver works through a plait from the footside and then is twisted twice to cross with the footside weaver. The trail is continued and the plait left out immediately.

At *o* the weaver works toward the footside until only the edge pair and two footside passive pairs remain. The pin is placed to the left of the weaver, the weaver is covered and both pairs become weavers. Continue to *p* where the pairs are joined and covered with cloth stitch. The right-hand pair becomes a passive and the left-hand pair continues as weaver.

Note that *q* is usually drawn in as a leaf but invariably worked as a tally using the weaver and plait pair to avoid the problem of pairs moving from one trail to the other with no obvious return point in a quickly executed regular pattern.

It is preferable to use a single pair at the base of the double ninepin to avoid too many pairs in the trail. A similar situation is shown in Fig. 43c.

Figure 101

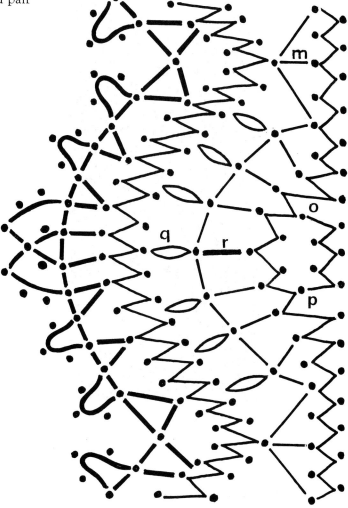

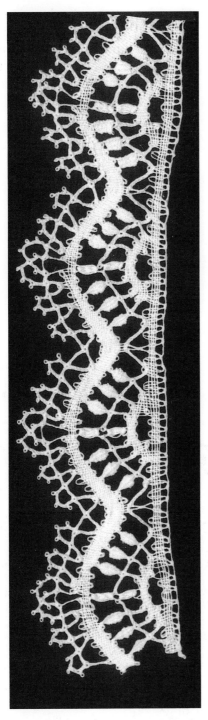

Figure 102

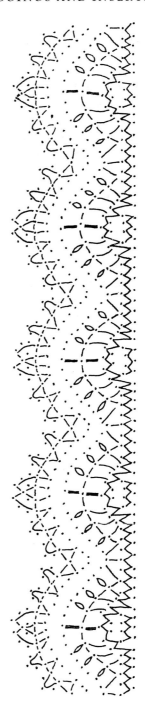

Figure 103

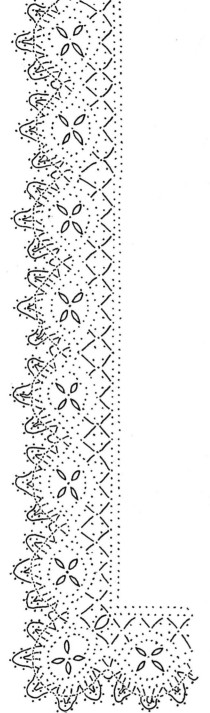

Pattern 27 Figs 104, 105 and 106

Two traditional prickings are identical other than the extra holes for double ninepin and the variation in the ground. (The fifth leaf in the corner is optional.) The photograph shows both results, the pricking can be adapted.

Headside The centre feature is double ninepin worked as Fig. 44c.

The ground The alternative ground with four picots at the plait crossing is described in Fig. 162 on page 108.

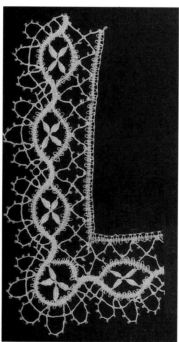

Figure 104

Figure 105 (*i* and *ii*)

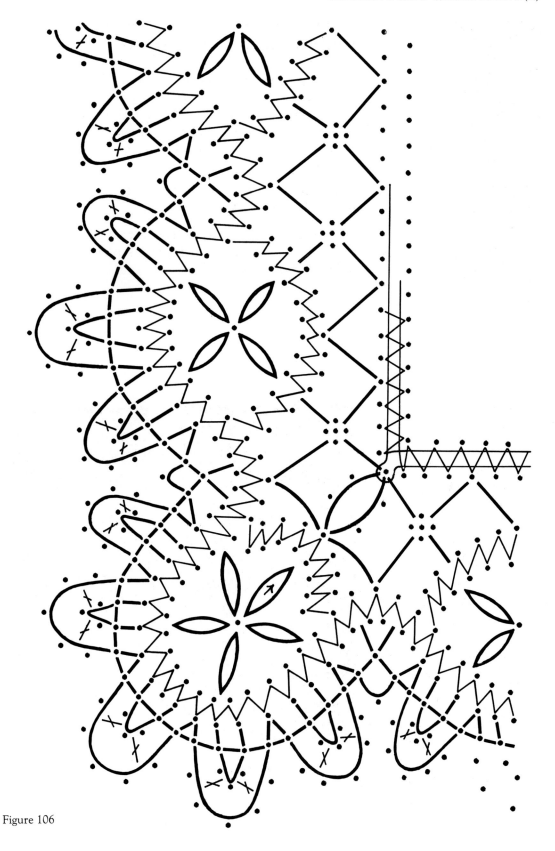

Figure 106

Pattern 28 Figs 107, 108 and 109

Refer to the diagram to clarify the method of crossing trails. Pairs are left out as indicated and Fig. 158a explains the working of the centre feature.

Headside The inner plait threads and the trail weaver work cloth stitch and two twists to link the headside plait to the trail at a, b and c. Alternatively it is very attractive to link with a tally.

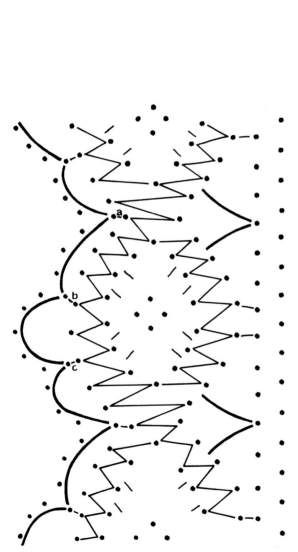

Figure 107

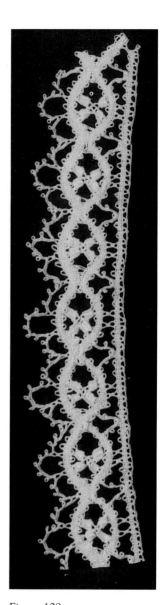

Figure 108

Figure 109

Pattern 29   Figs 110, 111 and 112

The diagram illustrates the working method. The feature in the ground at *u* is described in Fig. 161 on page 108. Additional pairs are required in the headside trail at the corner to work the leaves.

Figure 110

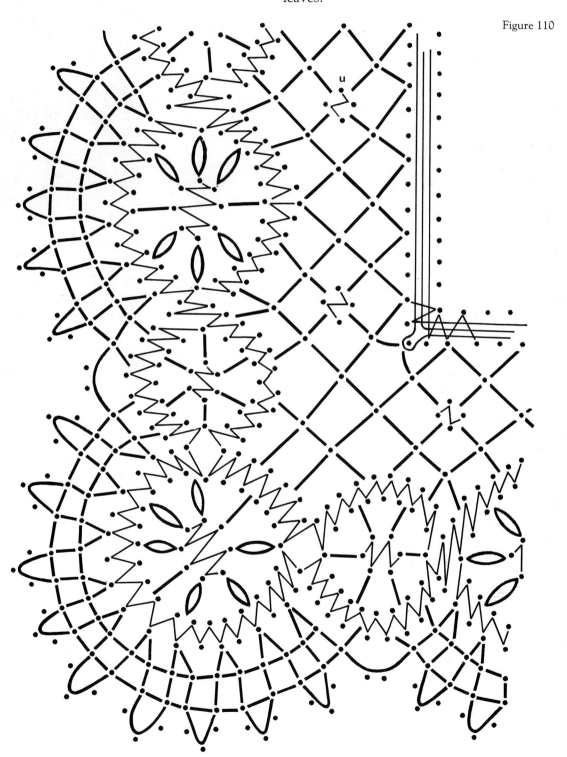

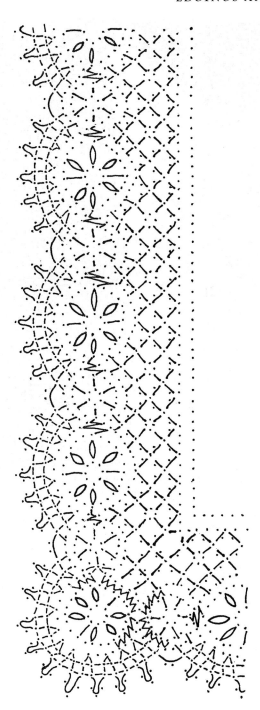

Figure 112

Figure 111 (*opposite*)

Pattern 30 Figs 113, 114 and 115

The dots across the diamond indicate that passive pairs are twisted at that point. Four additional pairs are required in the headside half-stitch trail for the extra leaves. Remember that these pairs can be discarded in the cloth diamond or the plaits but *not* within the half-stitch trail.

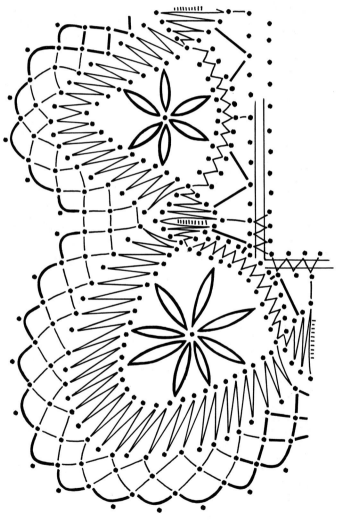

Figure 113   Figure 114

Figure 115 (*opposite*)

4

Patterns with point ground and honeycomb fillings

Some old patterns make a feature of point ground or honeycomb as the workers were familiar with these stitches in Bucks Point patterns. Simple torchon grounds were also used.

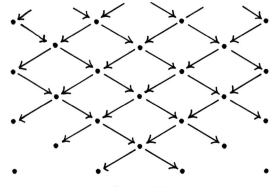

Figure 117

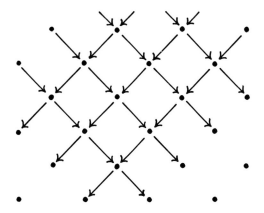

Figure 116

Torchon half stitch Fig. 116 Pairs enter diagonally from each side and work a half stitch; the pin is put in and covered with half stitch. Therefore rows should, as far as possible, be worked in diagonal lines.

Torchon cloth stitch and twist This is worked as the previous ground but cloth stitch and twist is worked before and after the pin. Alternatively cloth stitch and two twists may be used.

Point ground Fig. 117 Before a ground stitch is made, the pairs must be twisted three times. It is necessary to twist the pair as it comes from the trail, but as the ground

progresses the twists will be present from the previous stitches. Pairs come to the pin diagonally and work a stitch – cross and three twists; the pin is put in position but *not covered*. Work diagonally without covering pins.

Honeycomb Fig. 118 The angle of the pricking for honeycomb varies. Unlike Bucks Point it is frequently at 45° in Bedfordshire patterns. Throughout it is worked with two pairs making a honeycomb stitch – cross and two twists; the pin is put up and covered with honeycomb stitch. To understand the principle work as follows: two pairs work pin A, pairs are introduced to work the diagonal row, B, C, D, E, F and so on. The next row is worked G, H, J – there are spaces between the pins. The next row is continuous K, M, N, O, P. Note that pairs travel diagonally and vertically.

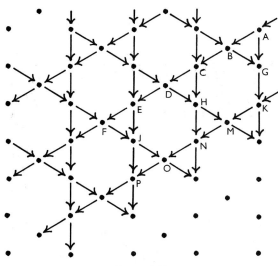

Figure 118

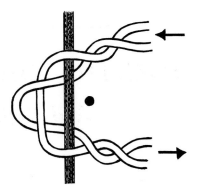

Figure 120

The pairs coming to the honeycomb ground from trails must be twisted twice before the ground is worked.

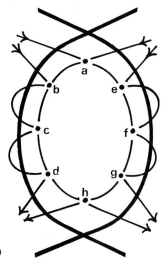

Figure 119

Honeycomb circles Fig. 119 The number of holes within the ring may vary, but Fig. 119 is a typical example used in the patterns in this section. Work pin *a*, normally using the inner pair from each plait. The left side pair from *a* travels to *b* to work honeycomb pin *b* with the other half of the plait. One pair remains within the circle, the other passes round the gimp, is twisted twice, returns round the gimp and is twisted twice more before working pin *c*. Refer to Fig.

120. It travels round the gimp again and works pin *d*. The other side is worked similarly and both pairs meet for pin *h*.

To achieve a pleasing result it is important to leave pairs out from the trails so that they enter the ground at the correct angle. Apart from honeycomb this will always be diagonally. In honeycomb certain pairs travel vertically.

Use of gimp threads These may be used to outline and emphasize a design. They also serve to hide unevenness and create the impression of a smooth curve. The thickness of gimp thread is at the discretion of the lacemaker and a study of old lace is recommended. For instance a thin gimp will be used to outline scrolls where the smooth line is more important than the sight of the gimp thread.

It may be placed around the design as in Bucks Point; half stitch flowers are usually surrounded with gimp thread. When the gimp emphasizes a smooth curve it is frequently laid alongside the outer passive thread; refer to Pattern 56.

Pattern 31 Figs 121, 122a and 123a

Refer to the top part of Fig. 121. To begin the half stitch edge use at least ten pairs and work cloth stitch and twist on each side of the edge pins to achieve a firm edge. Four of these pairs are required for plaits to work the honeycomb rings.

Work the first ring. Cross the gimp threads and continue to the right through the two pairs from ring 1 and the plait pairs from the footside. In ring 2 work pins *r* and *s*; now put in pin *t* and work another honeycomb stitch to cover it. Similarly put in pin *u* and cover with honeycomb. As the pinholes are close together the stitches will remain firm. One pair from *v* travels out round the gimp thread to work with the footside weaver and returns for pin *w*. Complete the ring.

Bring the gimp thread back to the centre and out to the left for ring 3. Work ring 3 as ring 2. One pair links with the half stitch trail at *y*. Cross the gimp threads and work ring 4. Note that the *same* gimp encloses rings 2 and 3.

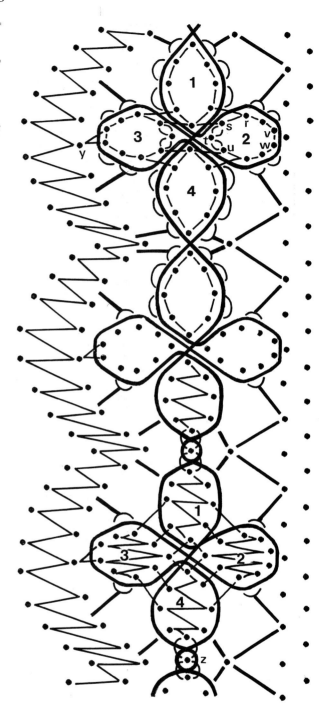

Figure 121

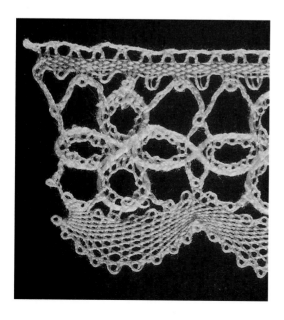

Figure 122a (detail)

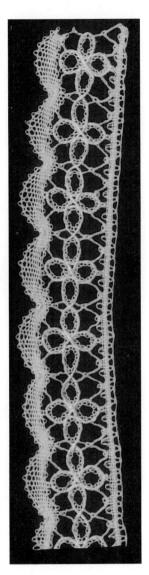

Figure 122a

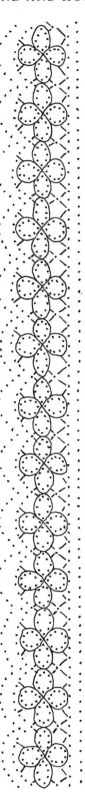

Figure 123a

Pattern 32   Figs 121, 122*b* and 123*b*

This is similar to Pattern 31 but two pairs
extra are required to begin half stitch ring 1.
On each side both pairs in the plait are
brought in at the same pin but left out
singly as shown.

Work the other rings in set order and cross
the gimps at the end of the fourth ring and
take them through the centre pairs as
shown. Work honeycomb stitch, pin *z* and
cover with honeycomb. Cross the gimp
threads and bring the pairs round the gimp
to begin ring 1 again.

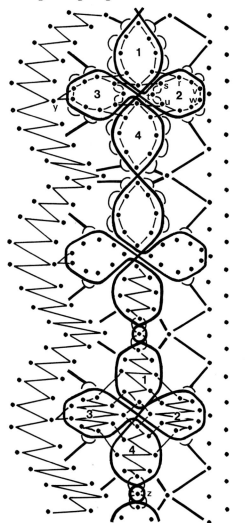

Figure 121

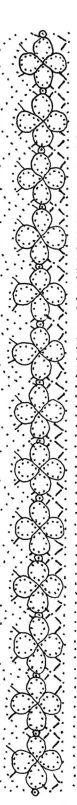

Figure 122*b*

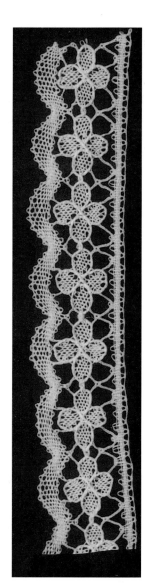

Figure 123*b*

Pattern 33 Figs 124, 125 and 126

The four-pin cloth feature in ground is described in Fig. 161. The gimp is overlapped at the end of the fourth ring and pairs laid back to be cut off when required for the next collection of rings.

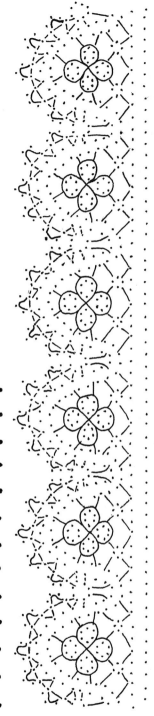

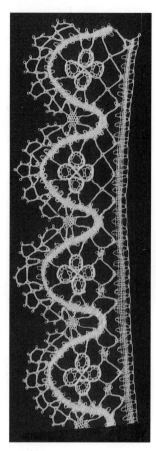

Figure 126

Figure 125

Figure 124

Pattern 34 Figs 127, 128 and 129

The flower centre ground is worked with
cloth stitch and two twists, pin, cloth stitch
and two twists. A pin is placed between the
plait pairs at *a*, and covered with cloth
stitch and two twists.

Leaf pairs at *f* are used as single threads.
The weaver from *e* is well twisted and
works cloth stitch and twist through the
leaf; it must again be well twisted before
working the corner ground pin *d*. It travels
back in the same way; pin *f* is used twice.
The footside weaver from *g* works similarly.
Six-plait crossings are worked at *y* and *z*.

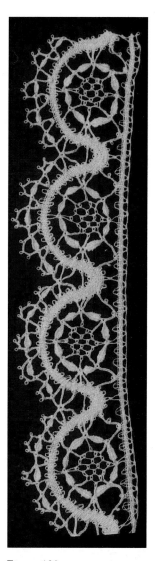

Figure 129

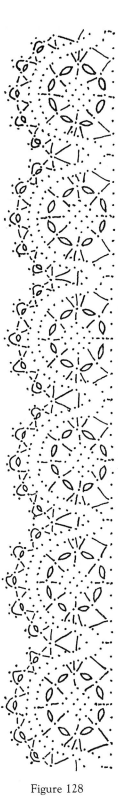

Figure 128

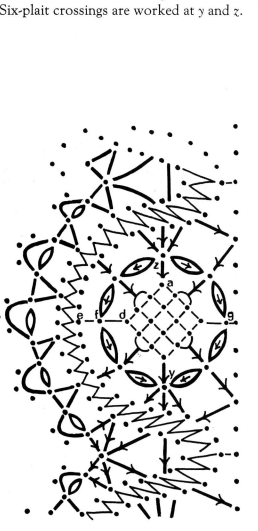

Figure 127

Pattern 35 Figs 130, 131 and 132*a* and *b*

The ground is worked with cloth and two twists before and after the pin. Honeycomb is worked within the cloth feature. Detailed Diagram 132*b* shows the use of the weaver and position of passive pairs.

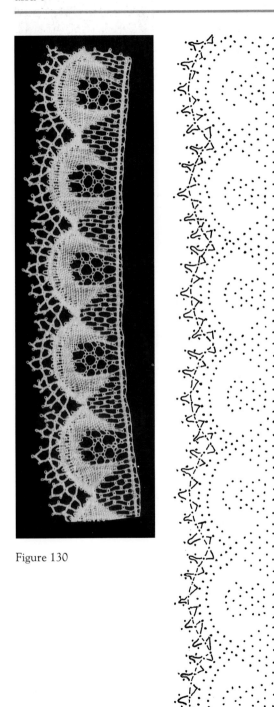

Figure 130

Figure 131

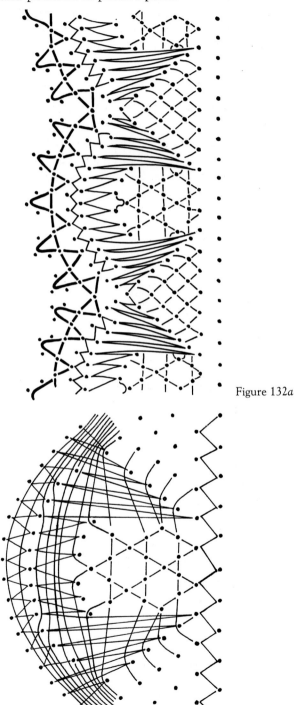

Figure 132*a*

Figure 132*b*

Pattern 36 Figs 133, 134 and 135

Ground The cloth stitch feature is described in Fig. 159 on page 107.

The cloth circle with hole No pairs enter or leave the circle at pins *a* and *b*. The weaver is twisted three times. The outer passive pairs are handled carefully to give a rounded effect at the point.

The trail Pairs are left out at *e* for the leaf and taken in at *f*. These pairs are carried in the trail and used in the same position each time.

Figure 133

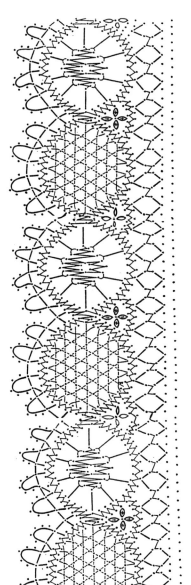

Figure 134

The filling Study honeycomb ground in Fig. 118. In order to maintain the vertical and diagonal lines, pairs are crossed with cloth stitch and two twists at *r*, *s* and *t* before the continuous row is worked. Similarly they are crossed at *u*, *v* and *w*. The weavers are marked on the diagram; there are no further problems.

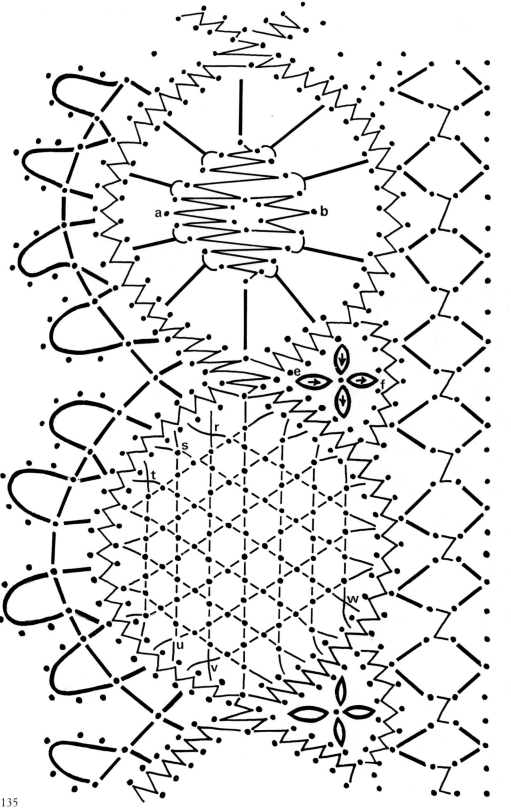

Figure 135

Pattern 37   Figs 136 and 137

The photograph shows the lace made with
different threads, 100/2 linen and 60/2 Brok
cotton, one more suited to table linen, the
other for a handkerchief. Care should be
taken to ensure good tension when using
the thicker thread. Picots are at the
discretion of the lacemaker.

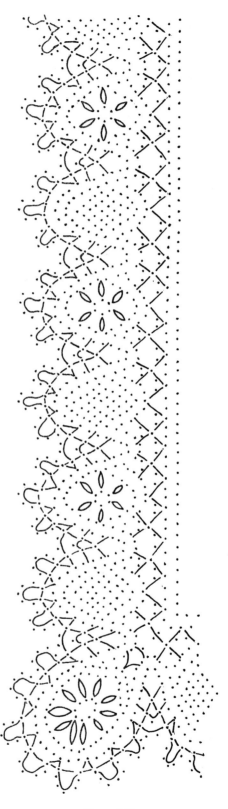

Figure 137 (detail)   Figure 136

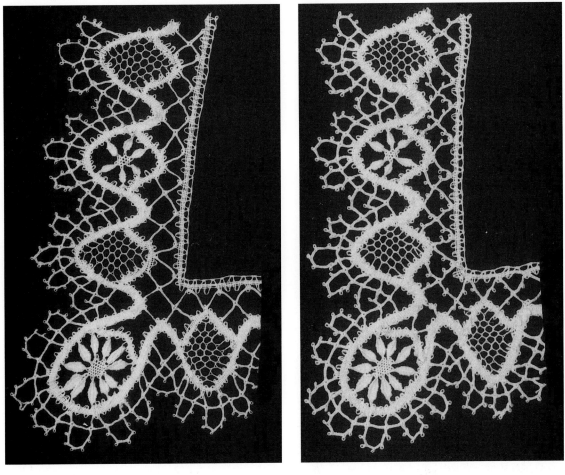

Figure 137 (*i* and *ii*)

Pattern 38 Figs 138, 139 and 140

In the past, square leaves were known as
plaits and consequently the ground as in
this pattern is always referred to as plaited
ground. See Fig. 158a and b on page 107.

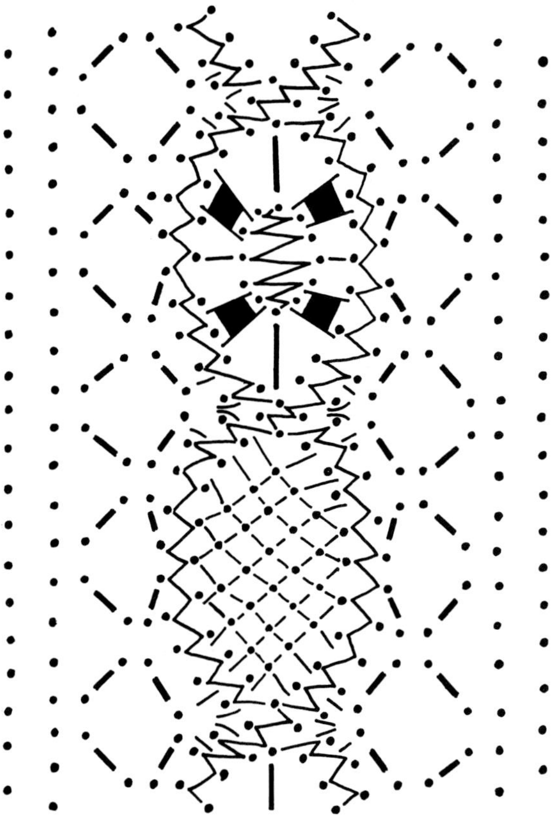

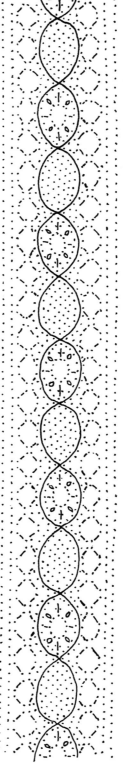

Figure 140

Figure 138

Figure 139

Pattern 39 Figs 141*a* and *b* and 142

Many old patterns have the large ninepin edge worked in fine thread. However, today, one is more inclined to choose a closer ninepin edge which may look less attractive but is easier to launder. Unless one is prepared to introduce and discard pairs within each head a fine thread is required to provide sufficient pairs for the point ground filling. Fig. 141*a* shows the working of the footside.

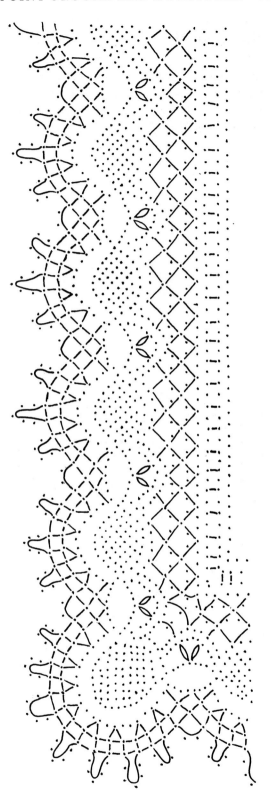

Figure 141*b*

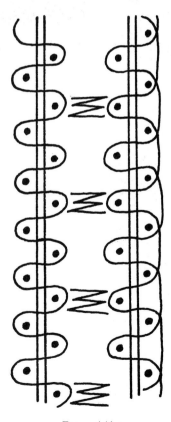

Figure 141*a*

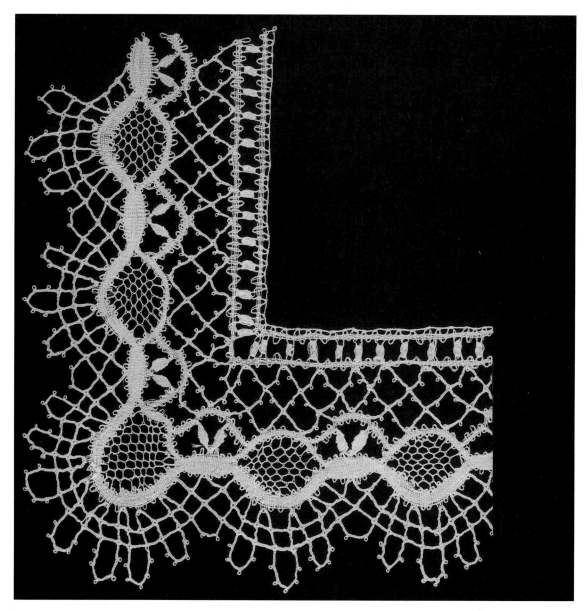

Figure 142

Pattern 40   Figs 143, 144 and 145

The headside is unusual. As the outer passive pair works cloth stitch through the plait pairs, it is twisted twice as a weaver, the pin is put up and the weaver returns to become outer passive again. This has not been indicated on the pricking as it may cause confusion when preparing the pricking.

At least four pairs must be introduced into the outer headside trail at the corner to provide pairs for the additional plaits. A cloth diamond – known as a mayflower – is worked in the corner honeycomb.

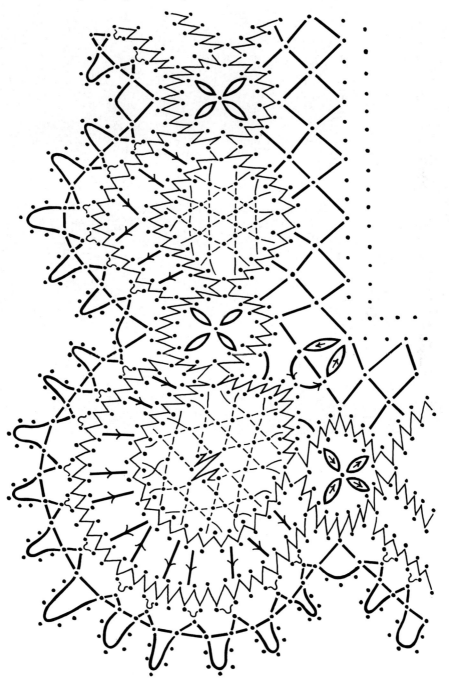

Figure 143

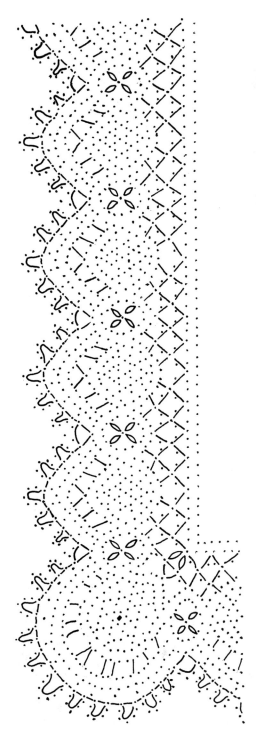

Figure 144

Figure 145

5

Collars, cuffs, yokes and edgings; working Lester and other pattern drafts

Bedfordshire lace extends beyond the simple repetitive edgings to collars, cuffs, caps, lappets and a wealth of more complicated yet exciting patterns. When working, practice and accumulated experience should be coupled with common sense and perseverance. Study the pricking and consider the finished result. Take every opportunity to study old lace – or illustrations of old lace. Where is a good position to start and where should the lace be completed for strength and neatness? Where will a join show least?

Always try to relate the current situation to one experienced previously. An enlarged copy of the pricking is invaluable – draw in weaver lines and plan how passive threads will be used in grounds or fillings. Remember that the number of pairs may vary according to the thread thickness and the tension of the lacemaker. Try out methods and ideas, and be willing to add and discard pairs as necessary. No two pieces of lace will be identical – however, techniques should be correct and worked in the traditional manner, the lace should appear attractive and it must be fit for the purpose intended. A collar should fit the neck and withstand regular laundering, whereas a picture should sit well within its frame and there should be no obvious ends to spoil the appearance.

The following photographs, Figs 146 – 155, offer the opportunity to examine old lace closely.

Figure 146

95

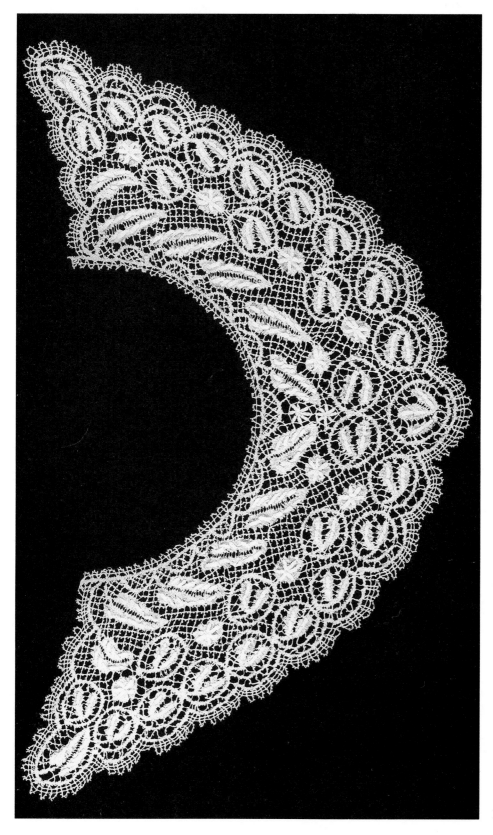

Figure 147

Figure 148

Figure 149

Figure 150

Figure 151

Figure 152

Figure 153

Figure 154

Figure 155

Pattern 41

The lower edging in Fig. 151 can be made using Pricking 156. The ground is explained in Fig. 161.

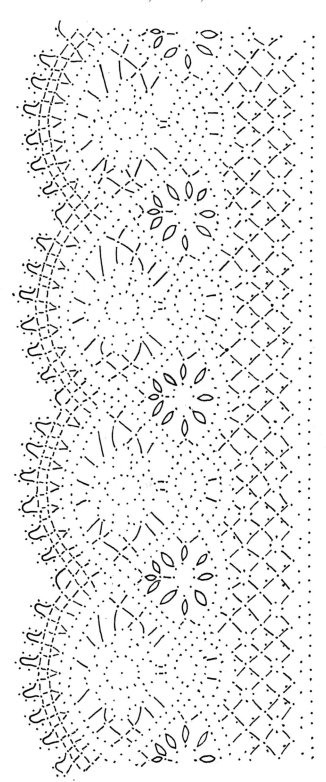

Figure 156

Pattern 42

Figure 157

Pricking 157 is similar to the collar, Fig. 148. However it is a more suitable shape for twentieth-century use; the ninepin around the neck edge may be omitted.

100mm

Techniques

Grounds

1. The most usual ground consists of plaits with or without picots and four-plait crossings; the collar in Fig. 147 is an excellent example. At a distance the plaits recede or are less noticeable whereas the leaf and trail design is more obvious. Occasionally the pairs are worked through each other with cloth stitch – see Fig. 150 (top).

2. Plaited ground, illustrated in Fig. 152 (centre), is not the ground described above. The confusion arises as the traditional name for the long square leaf was 'plait' (plaits were known as legs). Refer to Fig. 158 *a* and *b*. Work square leaves from *a* and *b*. Note the threads used for the weavers and the position in which they complete the leaves. Put in pins *q* and *r* to support them. Twist all pairs three times and cross with cloth stitch and three twists as shown. Put in pins *s* and *t*. Work two more leaves to *c* and *d*. Again note the position of the weaver at beginning and end.

Working in this way the weaver is not used until the leaves are anchored and therefore it helps to retain a well-shaped square leaf. It is linked to the footside as shown in Fig. 158*b*. The leaf pairs are twisted as usual. The right-hand pair works cloth stitch, pin, cloth stitch with the footside weaver. The footside pair works to the foot edge and back. The other pair, twisted three times, works cloth and three twists with the left-side leaf pair. This pair works with the footside weaver as described previously.

3. The ground in Fig. 149 (bottom) has the same hole arrangement as the previous pattern but is usually found interspersed with four-plait crossings. It may be worked in cloth stitch, or half stitch in black lace. Fig. 159 illustrates the method.

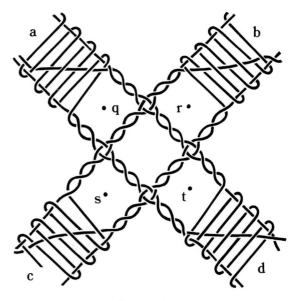

Figure 158*a*

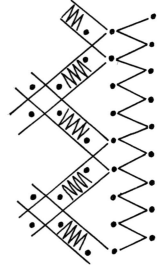

Figure 158*b*

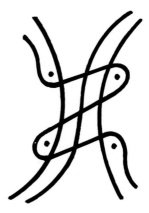

Figure 159

4. This may be used in ground but more often is used for flower fillings. Refer to Fig. 160. Plaits are made from x and y and pins a and b are put between the plait pairs. Centre pairs make the tally. Narrow square leaves are made from a and b to c and d. The centre pairs make a tally between c and d. Plaits are made to the next feature. When pins b and d are part of the footside the footside weaver is used to make the tally at ab and later at cd.

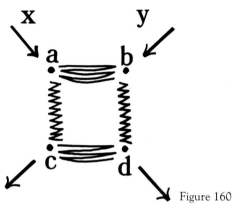

Figure 160

5. The hole arrangement used in grounds 2, 3 and 4 is different from that used in examples 5 and 6. Refer to lace in Fig. 151 (bottom) and the working diagram, Fig. 161. The diamond is worked in cloth stitch.

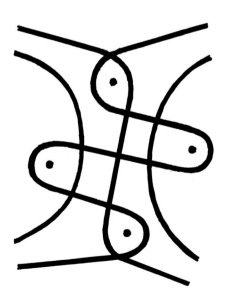

Figure 161

6. An identical hole arrangement is interpreted differently in the lace in Fig. 155 and the cuff in Fig. 154 where it appears immediately below the centre motif. The plait crossing is decorated with picots as in the Honiton Blossom filling. Refer to Fig. 162 and work as follows: Plait the left-hand plait to make a

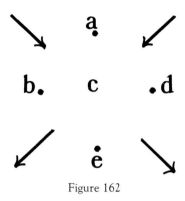

Figure 162

picot at a, work half stitch and a picot at b, work half stitch. Plait the right-hand plait almost to the centre position c and cloth stitch the pairs through each other. Sometimes a four-plait crossing is made and if this method is adopted it is necessary to add a hole at c. With the right-hand pair work half stitch and a picot at d, another half stitch and picot at e. Pairs from the same plait make all four picots. Continue. Today the Honiton method is used frequently and has become accepted. However the effect is different as it has a hole in the centre.

7. In Fig. 150 similar grounds are illustrated in the black lace (centre and bottom), and also in the metallic thread lace in Fig. 146. Refer to Fig. 163. Plaits are worked as shown by thick lines and cross at top and bottom of the oval. If firm thread is used or the space is confined, this is sufficient but if the thread is soft, additional twisted or plaited pairs are needed to retain the shape.

8. The circle is a feature frequently found in the more elaborate patterns and is illustrated in the collar in Fig. 153. Refer to Fig. 164 for the method of working. Normally the plait

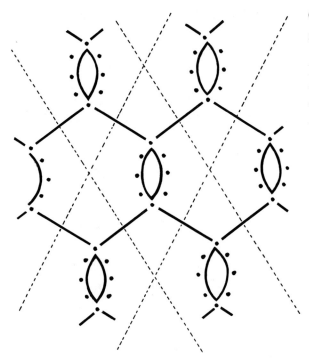

Figure 163

Cloth stitch leaves. Figs 165*a*, *b* and *c*.

Fig. 165*a*. A second weaver is introduced using the pair above the pinhole. When the weavers meet either a 'kiss' – crossing weavers – or a tally is worked.

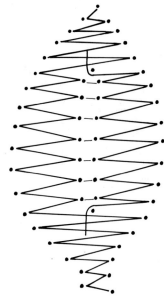

Figure 165*a*

Fig. 165*b*. When the leaf lies across the design, a second weaver is introduced but they do not meet. Passive pairs are left out on one side, twisted to accommodate the space and taken in on the other.

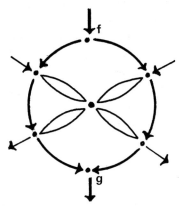

Figure 164

which enters at *f* and leaves at *g* is made with four pairs, to provide for plaits on each side of the circle.

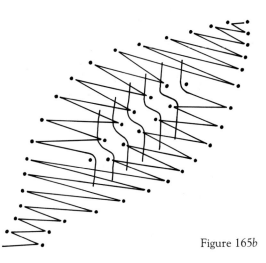

Figure 165*b*

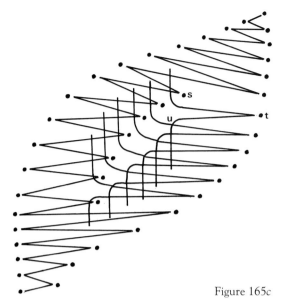

Figure 165c

To introduce extra pairs when starting a cloth feature along a straight line

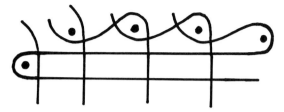

Figure 166a

Fig. 165c. When only one row of holes is present the weavers sometimes come together with cloth stitch and twist, pin, cloth stitch and twist. A better result is obtained when the cloth to one side of the vein is worked first. A second weaver is taken from s to the edge at t and back to position u where it loses its function as weaver. The passive pair adjacent to the pin is twisted twice and becomes a temporary weaver. As it returns to the vein it loses this function and the next passive pair becomes the weaver. It is important to manipulate the pairs to avoid unsightly holes. Sometimes the last stitch worked by the returning weaver is worked cross, twist, cross, twist, cross to hold it more firmly in position.

Fig. 166a. To introduce one pair at each pin hang pairs behind the work. Take the weaver through a pair, put up the pin and cover. Remove the support pin. The new pair works through the next hanging pair and the process is repeated.

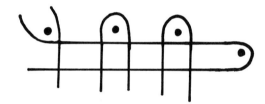

Figure 166b

Fig. 166b. To introduce two pairs at each pin, hang two pairs round the pin, twist one side three times and weave across the work.

To remove excess pairs when finishing a cloth stitch feature along a straight line

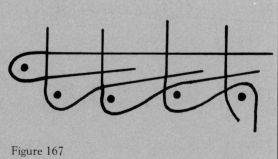

Fig. 167. Take the weaver back through at least two passive pairs. The next pin is put to the side of the next passive pair which works back through at least two pairs. Continue.

Figure 167

Pattern 43 Figs 168, 169 and 170

The square leaf at *s* provides passive pairs
for the outer trail; the existing passive pairs
pass through them and make the square leaf
at *t*. From the distance it creates the illusion
of crossed trails.

Figure 168

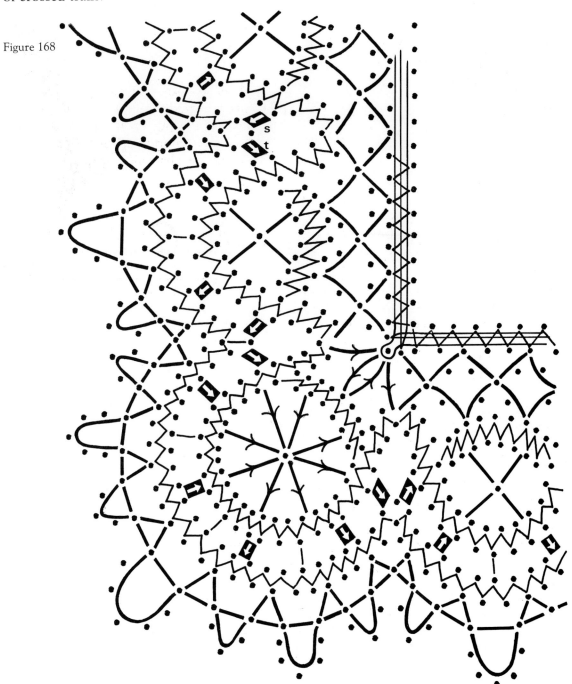

Figure 169

Figure 170

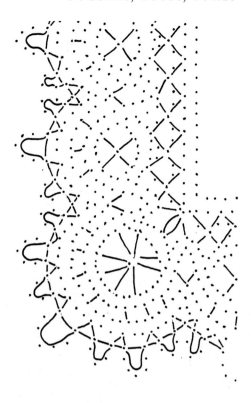

Figure 169 (detail)

Pattern 44 Figs 171 and 172

The use of weaver pairs to make the tallies allows the passive pairs in the headside trail to remain the same throughout.

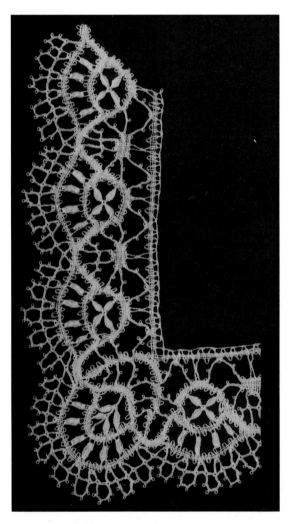

Figure 171

Figure 172

Pattern 45 Figs 173 and 174

The importance of good tension between the oval cloth features cannot be overemphasized. The ground cloth diamond is described in Fig. 161. Note the choice of plaits and leaves in the corner.

Figure 173

Figure 174

Pattern 46 Figs 175, 176 and 177

Originally these pieces were used for small collars but today they are used for cuffs. It is difficult to explain the neat beginning but refer to the diagram. Four pairs are laid across the pillow, two either side of pin *e*. Four threads are plaited to begin the ninepin edge. Pin *f* is put in position and two pairs hung round it. The right pair from *e* is laid to the right of the pairs on *f*. This pair and adjacent pair work cloth and two twists. Two pairs are added similarly at pin *g*.

Two pairs are laid either side of *y* and a plait is made to *h*, a pin is placed between the plait pairs and covered with cloth stitch. From pin *y*, one pair weaves to *j* where two extra pairs are joined in for the ninepin plait. The other pair becomes a footside passive. Pairs for plaits and leaves, for example at *r* and *s*, are joined in as necessary.

To complete the piece the pairs are taken into the headside trail and discarded. Eventually both trails join together.

NOTE: Raised tallies may be worked over the leaves as in Pattern 47.

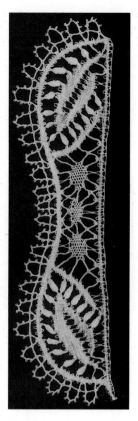

Figure 176

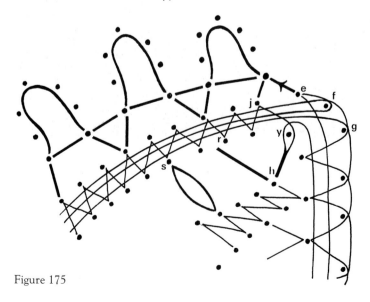

Figure 175

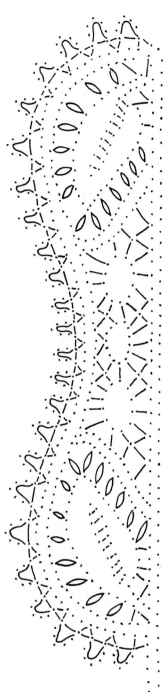

Figure 177

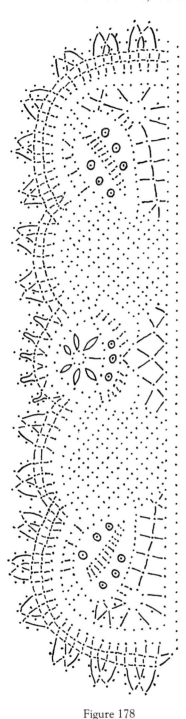

Figure 178

Pattern 47   Figs 178, 179 and 180

Hang four pairs round each of two pins and
use the pairs to the inner side of the pins to
work the four-plait crossing at *e*. Two plaits
are made in preparation for the double
ninepin edge and the other four pairs are
used as shown in the diagram. Pairs at *f* and
g are introduced as in the previous pattern.
The appropriate pairs from *e* and *g* work
through passive pairs to make a cloth stitch
before and after pin *h*. They become trail
and footside weaver pairs. Continue to add
pairs according to the diagram. All
techniques have been explained previously.

Figure 179

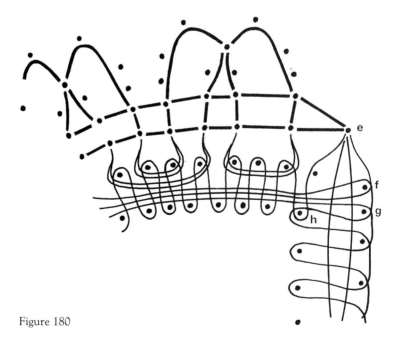

Figure 180

Pattern 48 Figs 181a and b, 182 and 183

Lay two pairs either side of pin e. The four threads to the back of the pillow work the plait and picots to y. Four pairs are hung from a support pin and the threads to one side of the pin are used with the plait pairs to make a four-plait crossing at y. Plait in both directions. Hang four pairs round pin f and work cloth stitch and two twists with the pairs to the right of the pin; twist all pairs twice. Place two pairs round pin g and the edge pair to the right of these. Twist the left-hand pair twice and work cloth stitch and two twists with the right-hand pairs. One additional pair is added at h. Pairs are added for plait and trail as shown at m and n. One additional weaver pair is added at n.

Fig. 181b shows the use of pairs for the flower feature.

To complete the collar, pairs are absorbed into the headside trail and then discarded. The ninepin pairs are plaited together and eventually sewn under the footside trail. Continue the footside trail, this can be folded back and the ends hidden securely inside.

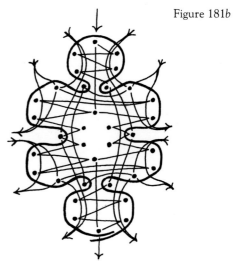

Figure 181b

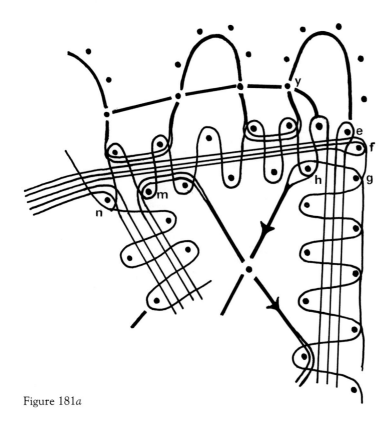

Figure 181a

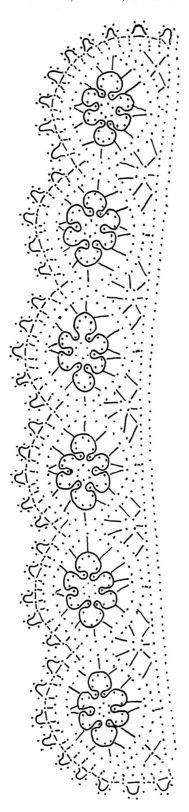

Figure 182

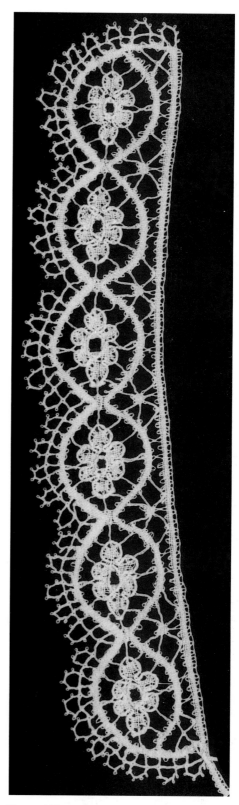

Figure 183

Pattern 49 Figs 184 and 185

The cuffs complement the edging in Pattern 23; refer to Fig. 141*a* for the footside.

Figure 184

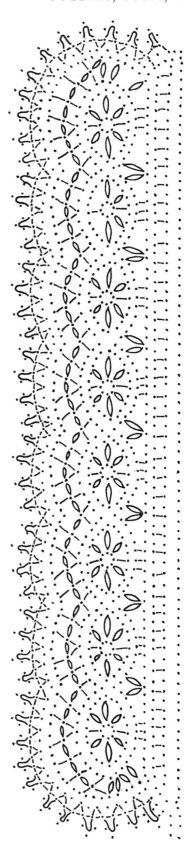

Figure 185

Pattern 50 Figs 186 and 187

NOTE: The pricking should be enlarged, the scale is shown. The lace to be used as a yoke on blouse or negligee was popular a century ago and may well prove to be an interesting alternative to the collar. A narrow edging of the required length should be worked first to avoid an unsightly join. The photograph for Pattern 51 will clarify the method of starting the lace.

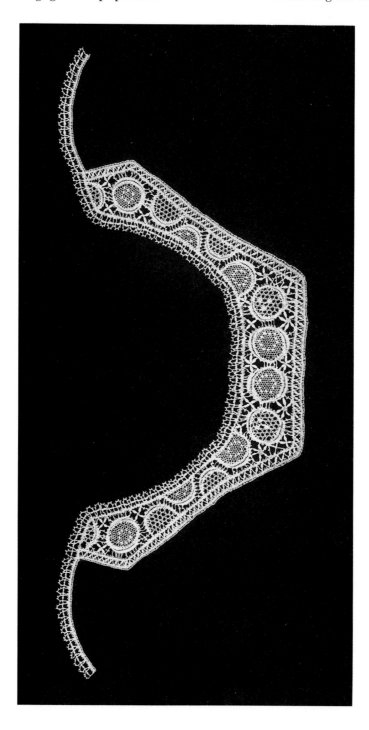

Figure 186

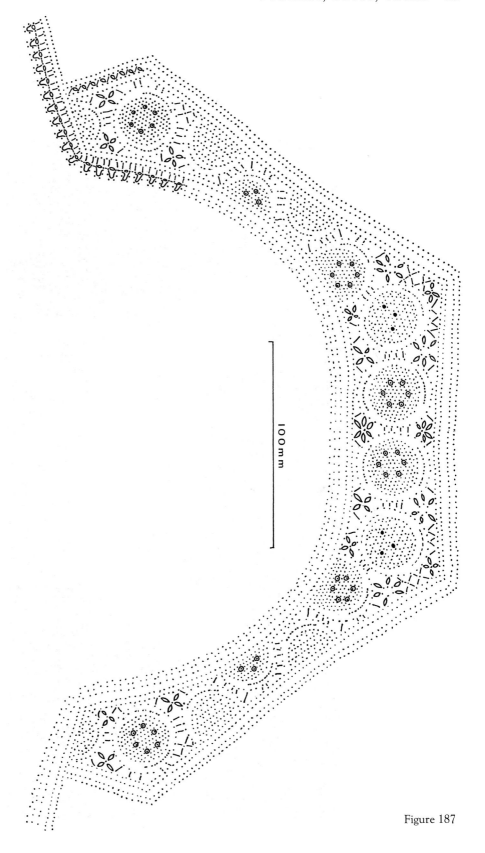

100mm

Figure 187

Pattern 51 Figs 188 and 189

The pattern should be enlarged.

Figure 188 (detail)

Figure 188

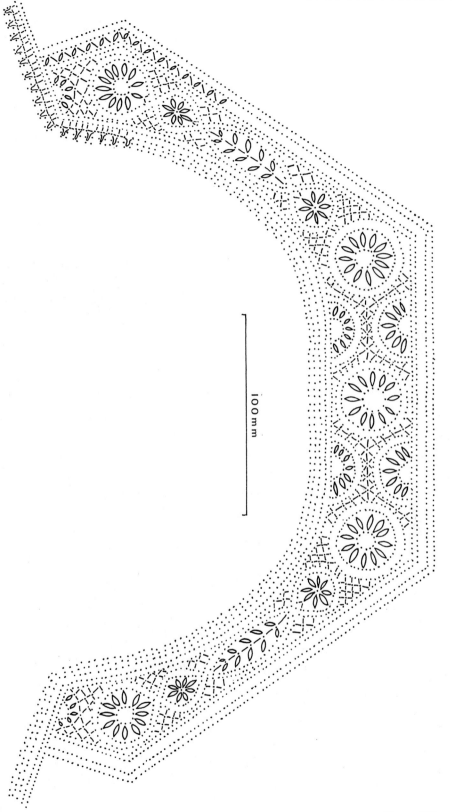

100mm

Figure 189

Pattern 52 Figs 190 and 191

The collar pricking, inscribed *19th August 1863, 3 dozen*, indicates that the lace was made to be sold. Today no one would be willing to make 36 identical collars! The old collar, worked in linen thread, has been washed and worn and is too small for use today. A linen floss outlines the scalloped headside and is carried as a footside passive. It was used to replace the edge thread, so that cloth stitch could be worked quickly across the trail. Also notice that for the third scallop in each head, both sets of plait pairs are taken out to provide pairs for the outer edge to avoid unnecessary thickness when pairs enter the main trail.

The original size is indicated on the pricking but it is so fine that it can be enlarged without spoiling the appearance.

Figure 190

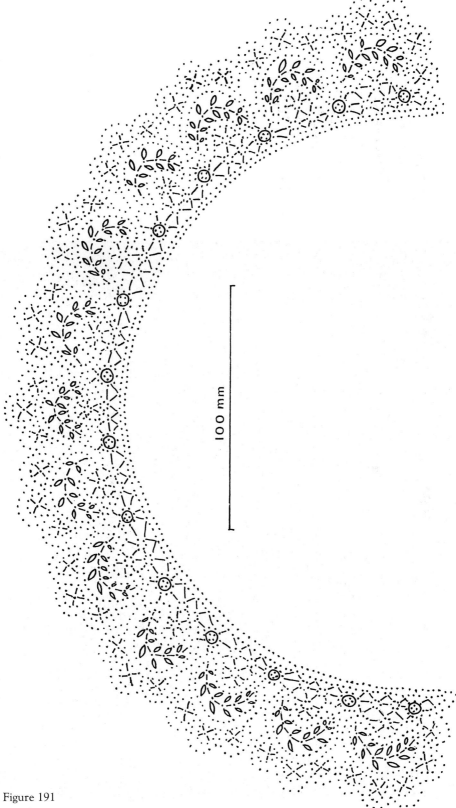

100 mm

Figure 191

Pattern 53 Figs 192 and 193

This pattern, an adaptation of the previous pattern, should be enlarged.

To make the second piece the lace should be worked with the footside on the left.

Figure 192

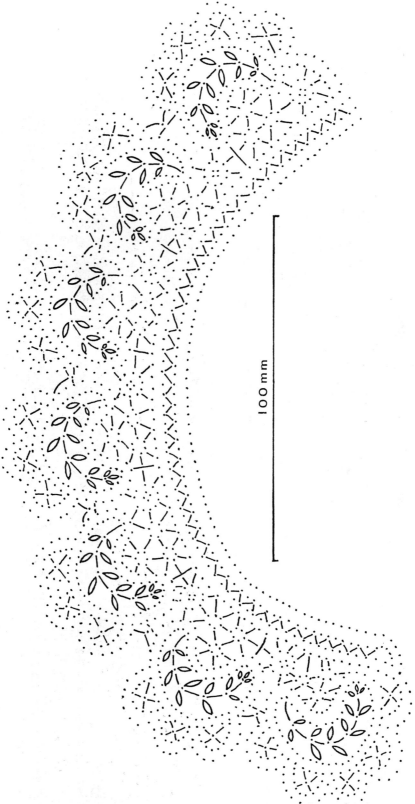

100 mm

Figure 193

Pattern 54   Figs 194 and 195

The pricking should be enlarged.

The lace is started at the outer edge with one circle and crossing trails worked in both directions. When the trail enters the footside (neck edge) trail, pairs are discarded as necessary.

To complete the collar work the crossing trails back to the neck edge. The pairs from the straight trail from the point are worked through the neck edge pairs; the trail is continued for ½in. (5 mm). When the outer edge trail and the neck edge trail meet, plait the pairs from the shorter trail tightly together. Remove a few pins from this trail and lay the trail to one side so that four pinholes more can be worked for the other trail. Similarly plait these threads tightly. When the lace is removed from the pillow the trail should be folded back to achieve an almost invisible join. The short trail should be folded back to partially cover the plaits. Strength is all-important as a collar requires frequent laundering.

Figure 194

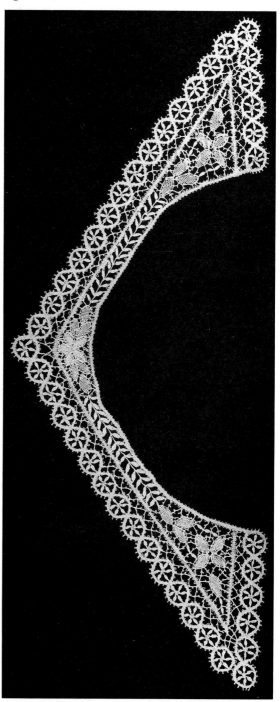

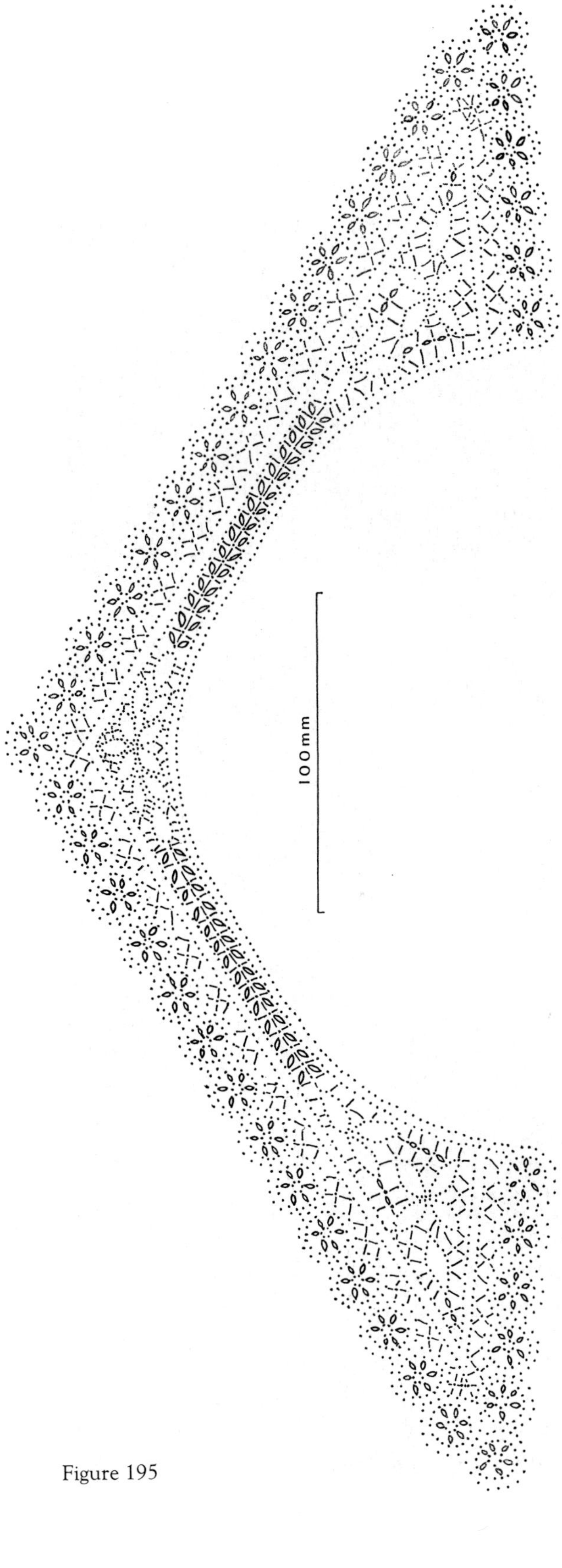

100mm

Pattern Drafts

Among the old pattern drafts there are very attractive designs inscribed *Lester*, *Clarke*, *Allen* and *Marshall*. Investigation and study are needed to understand the intricacies and develop the skills to make these laces once again. Patience and a willingness to experiment can provide hours of pleasure and a feeling of satisfaction. The experienced Bucks Point lace worker will find that a knowledge of working floral patterns will facilitate the working of these. Indeed, very similar designs can be found with plaited or point ground.

The following selection will serve as an introduction to this rather specialized lace. The diagrams are intended to offer a suggestion for working the cloth stitch features. Alternative methods are equally acceptable. It is important to introduce pairs into the cloth at the correct angle and leave them out similarly. D.M.C. Retors d'Alsace no. 50 thread is suitable.

Figure 195

Pattern 55 Figs 196, 197 and 198

From a Lester pattern draft.

Sufficient passive pairs should be included
in the headside trail to ensure that the
picots remain close to the gimp thread.

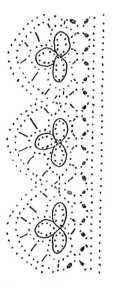

Figure 197

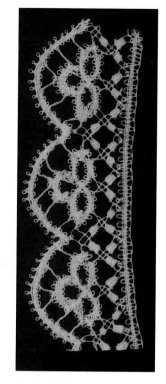

Figure 198

Figure 196

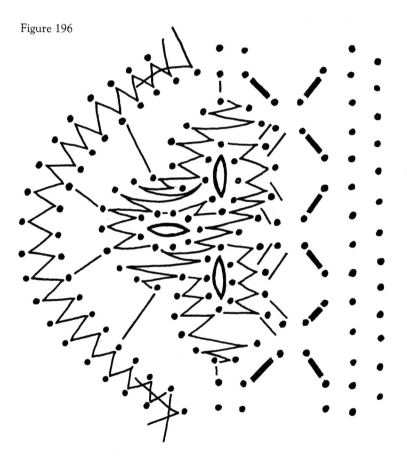

Pattern 56 Figs 199*a* and *b*, 200 and 201

From a Clarke pattern draft.

Fig. 199*b* shows the method of working a nook pin, as required at *z*. The weavers from the outer edge of the bell and the picot edge are worked together with cloth stitch and twist.

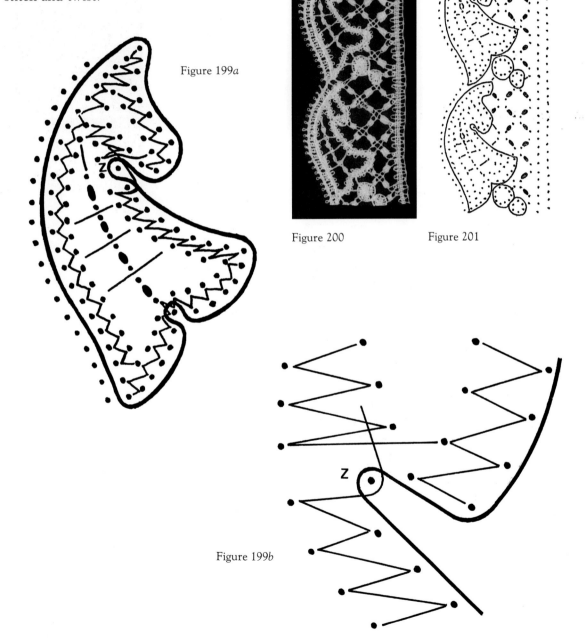

Figure 199*a*

Figure 200

Figure 201

Figure 199*b*

Pattern 57 Figs 202, 203 and 204

From a Clarke pattern draft.

Fig. 203 should be turned upside down to work the feature on the left side of the insertion. The weaver is twisted to the side of the pin but not between cloth and gimp thread.

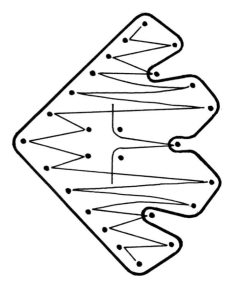

Figure 203

Figure 204

Figure 202

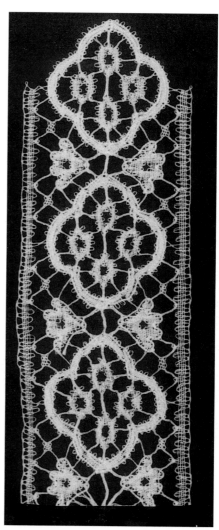

Pattern 58   Figs 205, 206 and 207 *a* and *b*

From a Marshall pattern draft.

The nook pins are worked as shown at R in Fig. 207*b*. The weaver loses its function and becomes a passive pair. Two pairs work S and one becomes the new weaver. Pin T is put up between the passive pairs and the pin is covered with cloth stitch and two twists. These pairs cross the gimps for use in the cloth below.

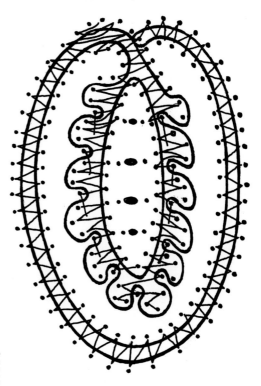

Figure 207*a*

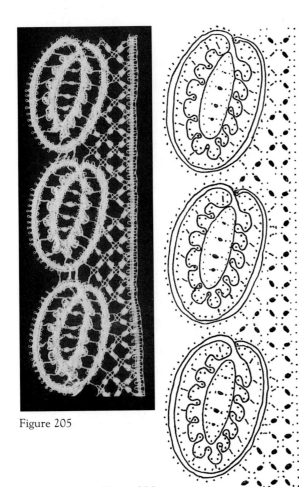

Figure 205

Figure 206

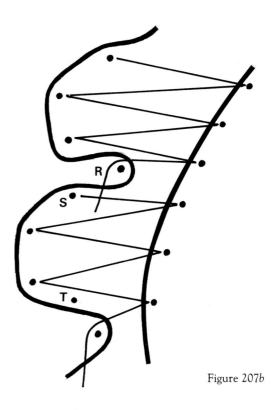

Figure 207*b*

Pattern 59 Figs 208 and 209

From a Lester pattern draft.

The lace has been turned over to show the right side.

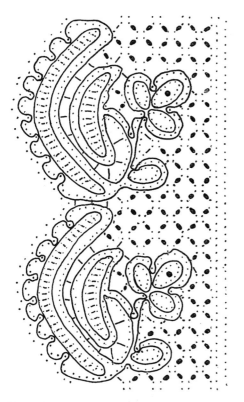

Figure 208

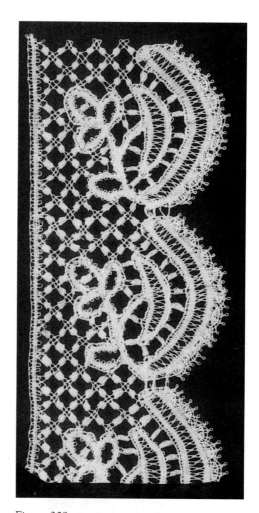

Figure 209

Pattern 60 Figs 210 and 211

The lace is old and made from a pricking
very similar to the pattern draft inscribed
Allen.

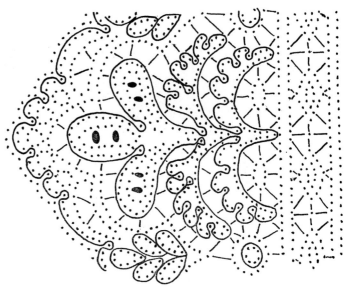

Figure 211

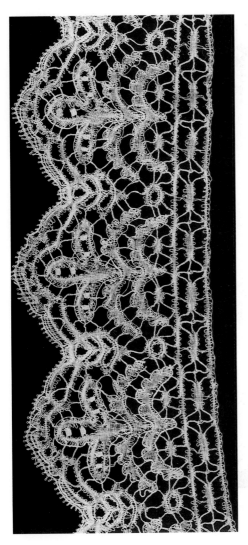

Figure 210

Suppliers and sources of information

Books

ENGLAND
The following are stockists of the complete Batsford/Dryad Press range:

AVON
Bridge Bookshop
7 Bridge Street
Bath BA2 4AS

Waterstone & Co.
4–5 Milsom Street
Bath BA1 1DA

BEDFORDSHIRE
Arthur Sells
Lane Cover
49 Pedley Lane
Clifton
Shefford SG17 5QT

BUCKINGHAMSHIRE
J. S. Sear
Lacecraft Supplies
8 Hillview
Sherington MK16 9NJ

CAMBRIDGESHIRE
Dillons the Bookstore
Sidney Street
Cambridge

CHESHIRE
Lynn Turner
Church Meadow Crafts
7 Woodford Road
Winsford

CORNWALL
Creative Books
22A River Street
Truro TR1 2SJ

DEVON
Creative Crafts & Needlework
18 High Street
Totnes TQ9 5NP

Honiton Lace Shop
44 High Street
Honiton EX14 8PJ

DORSET
F. Herring & Sons
27 High West Street
Dorchester DT1 1UP

Tim Parker (*mail order*)
124 Corhampton Road
Boscombe East
Bournemouth BH6 5NZ

Christopher Williams
19 Morrison Avenue
Parkstone
Poole BH17 4AD

DURHAM
Lacemaid
6, 10 & 15 Stoneybeck
Bishop Middleham
DL17 9BL

GLOUCESTERSHIRE
Southgate Handicrafts
63 Southgate Street
Gloucester GL1 1TX

Waterstone & Company
89–90 The Promenade
Cheltenham GL50 1NB

HAMPSHIRE
Creative Crafts
11 The Square
Winchester SO23 9ES

Doreen Gill
14 Barnfield Road
Petersfield GU31 4DR

Larkfield Crafts
4 Island Cottages
Mapledurwell
Basingstoke RG23 2LU

Needlestyle
24–26 West Street
Alresford

Ruskins
27 Bell Street
Romsey

ISLE OF WIGHT
Busy Bobbins
Unit 7
Scarrots Lane
Newport PO30 1JD

KENT
The Handicraft Shop
47 Northgate
Canterbury CT1 1BE

Hatchards
The Great Hall
Mount Pleasant Road
Tunbridge Wells

LONDON
W. & G. Foyle Ltd
113–119 Charing Cross Road
WC2H 0EB

Hatchards
187 Piccadilly W1V 9DA

MIDDLESEX
Redburn Crafts
Squires Garden Centre
Halliford Road
Upper Halliford
Shepperton TW17 8RU

NORFOLK
Alby Lace Museum
Cromer Road
Alby
Norwich NR11 7QE

Jane's Pincushions
Taverham Craft Unit 4
Taverham Nursery Centre
Fir Covert Road
Taverham
Norwich NR8 6HT

Waterstone & Company Ltd
30 London Street
Norwich NR2 1LD

NORTH YORKSHIRE
Craft Basics
9 Gillygate
York

Shireburn Lace
Finkle Court
Finkle Hill
Sherburn in Elmet LS25 6EB

The Craft House
23 Bar Street
Scarborough YO13 9QE

NORTHAMPTONSHIRE
Denis Hornsby
149 High Street
Burton Latimer
Kettering NN15 5RL

SOMERSET
Bridge Bookshop
62 Bridge Street
Taunton TA1 1UD

STAFFORDSHIRE
J. & J. Ford (*mail order & lace days only*)
October Hill
Upper Way
Upper Longdon
Rugeley WS15 1QB

SUSSEX
Waterstone & Company Ltd
120 Terminus Road
Eastbourne

WARWICKSHIRE
Christine & David Springett
21 Hillmorton Road
Rugby CV22 6DF

WEST MIDLANDS
Needlewoman
21 Needles Alley
off New Street
Birmingham B2 5AG

WEST YORKSHIRE
Sebalace
Waterloo Mill
Howden Road
Silsden BD20 0HA

George White Lacemaking Supplies
40 Heath Drive
Boston Spa LS23 6PB

Just Lace
Lacemaker Supplies
14 Ashwood Gardens
Gildersome
Leeds LS27 7AS

Jo Firth
58 Kent Crescent
Lowtown, Pudsey
Leeds LS28 9EB

WILTSHIRE
Everyman Bookshop
5 Bridge Street
Salisbury SP1 2ND

SCOTLAND
Embroidery Shop
51 William Street
Edinburgh
Lothian EH3 7LW

Waterstone & Company Ltd
236 Union Street
Aberdeen AB1 1TN

WALES
Bryncraft Bobbins (*mail order*)
B. J. Phillips
Pantglas
Cellan
Lampeter
Dyfed SA48 8JD

Hilkar Lace Suppliers
33 Mysydd Road
Landore
Swansea

DEVON
Honiton Lace Shop
44 High Street
Honiton EX14 8PJ

DORSET
Frank Herring & Sons
27 High West Street
Dorchester DT1 1UP

Tim Parker (*mail order, general and bobbins*)
124 Corhampton Road
Boscombe East
Bournemouth BH6 5NZ

ESSEX
Needlework
Ann Bartleet
Bucklers Farm
Coggeshall CO6 1SB

GLOUCESTERSHIRE
T. Brown (*bobbins*)
Temple Lane Cottage
Littledean
Cinderford

Chosen Crafts Centre
46 Winchcombe Street
Cheltenham GL52 2ND

HAMPSHIRE
Busy Bobbins
Unit 7
Scarrots Lane
Newport IOW
PO30 1JD

Larkfield Crafts (*bobbins*)
Hilary Ricketts
4 Island Cottages
Mapledurwell
Basingstoke RG23 2LU

Needlestyle
24–26 West Street
Alresford

Newnham Lace Equipment (*lace pillows*)
15 Marlowe Close
Basingstoke RG24 9DD

Richard Viney (*bobbins*)
Unit 7
Port Royal Street
Southsea PO5 3UD

KENT
The Handicraft Shop
47 Northgate
Canterbury CT1 1BE

Denis Hornsby
25 Manwood Avenue
Canterbury CT2 7AH

Frances Iles
73 High Street
Rochester ME1 1LX

LANCASHIRE
Malcolm J. Fielding (*bobbins*)
2 Northern Terrace
Moss Lane
Silverdale LA5 0ST

LINCOLNSHIRE
Ken and Pat Schultz
Whynacres
Shepeau Stow
Whaplode Drove
Spalding PE12 0TU

MERSEYSIDE
Hayes & Finch
Head Office & Factory
Hanson Road
Aintree
Liverpool L9 9BP

MIDDLESEX
Redburn Crafts
Squires Garden Centre
Halliford Road
Upper Halliford
Shepperton TW17 8RU

NORFOLK
Alby Lace Museum
Cromer Road
Alby
Norwich NR11 7QE

Jane's Pincushions
Taverham Craft Unit 4
Taverham Nursery Centre
Fir Covert Road
Taverham
Norwich NR8 6HT

George Walker
The Corner Shop
Rickinghall, Diss

NORTH HUMBERSIDE
Teazle Embroideries
35 Boothferry Road
Hull

Equipment

UNITED KINGDOM

BEDFORDSHIRE
A. Sells
49 Pedley Lane
Clifton
Shefford SG17 5QT

BERKSHIRE
Chrisken Bobbins
26 Cedar Drive
Kingsclere RG15 8TD

BUCKINGHAMSHIRE
J. S. Sear
Lacecraft Supplies
8 Hillview
Sherington MK16 9NJ

Sizelands
1 Highfield Road
Winslow MK10 3QU

SMP
4 Garners Close
Chalfont St Peter SL9 0HB

CAMBRIDGESHIRE
Josie and Jeff Harrison (*pillows*)
Walnut Cottage
Winwick
Huntingdon PE17 5PP

Heffers Graphic Shop (*matt coloured transparent adhesive film*)
26 King Street
Cambridge CB1 1LN

Spangles
Carole Morris
Cashburn Lane
Burwell CB5 0ED

CHESHIRE
Lynn Turner
Church Meadow Crafts
7 Woodford Road
Winsford

NORTH YORKSHIRE
The Craft House
23 Bar Street
Scarborough

Shireburn Lace
Finkle Court
Finkle Hill
Sherburn in Elmet LS25 6EB

Stitchery
Finkle Street
Richmond

NORTHAMPTONSHIRE
Denis Hornsby
149 High Street
Burton Latimer
Kettering NN15 5RL

SOUTH YORKSHIRE
D. H. Shaw
47 Lamor Crescent
Thrushcroft
Rotherham S66 9QD

STAFFORDSHIRE
J. & J. Ford (*mail order and lace days only*)
October Hill
Upper Way
Upper Longdon
Rugeley WS15 1QB

SUFFOLK
A. R. Archer (*bobbins*)
The Poplars
Shetland
near Stowmarket IP14 3DE

Mary Collins (*linen by the metre, and made up articles of church linen*)
Church Furnishings
St Andrews Hall
Humber Doucy Lane
Ipswich IP4 3BP

E. & J. Piper (*silk embroidery and lace thread*)
Silverlea
Flax Lane
Glemsford CO10 7RS

SURREY
Needle and Thread
80 High Street
Horsell
Woking GU21 4SZ

Needlestyle
5 The Woolmead
Farnham GU9 7TX

SUSSEX
Southern Handicrafts
20 Kensington Gardens
Brighton BN1 4AC

WARWICKSHIRE
Christine & David Springett
21 Hillmorton Road
Rugby CV22 5DF

WEST MIDLANDS
Framecraft
83 Hampstead Road
Handsworth Wood
Birmingham B2 1JA

The Needlewoman
21 Needles Alley
off New Street
Birmingham B2 5AE

Stitches
Dovehouse Shopping Parade
Warwick Road
Olton, Solihull

WEST YORKSHIRE
Jo Firth
Lace Marketing &
    Needlecraft Supplies
58 Kent Crescent
Lowtown
Pudsey LS28 9EB

Just Lace
Lacemaker Supplies
14 Ashwood Gardens
Gildersome
Leeds LS27 7AS

Sebalace
Waterloo Mills
Howden Road
Silsden BD20 0HA

George White Lacemaking Supplies
40 Heath Drive
Boston Spa LS23 6PB

WILTSHIRE
Doreen Campbell (*frames and mounts*)
Highcliff
Bremilham Road
Malmesbury SN16 0DQ

SCOTLAND
Christine Riley
53 Barclay Street
Stonehaven
Kincardineshire

Peter & Beverley Scarlett
Strupak
Hill Head
Cold Wells, Ellon
Grampian

WALES
Bryncraft Bobbins
B. J. Phillips
Pantglas
Cellan
Lampeter
Dyfed SA48 8JD

Hilkar Lace Suppliers
33 Mysydd Road
Landore
Swansea

AUSTRALIA
Australian Lace magazine
P.O. Box 1291
Toowong
Queensland 4066

Dentelles Lace Supplies
c/o Betty Franks
39 Lang Terrace
Northgate 4013
Brisbane
Queensland

The Lacemaker
724a Riversdale Road
Camberwell 3124

Spindle and Loom
83 Longueville Road
Lane Cove
NSW 2066

Tulis Crafts
201 Avoca Street
Randwick
NSW 2031

BELGIUM
't Handwerkhuisje
Katelijnestraat 23
8000 Bruges

Kantcentrum
Balstraat 14
8000 Bruges

Manufacture Belge de Dentelle
6 Galerie de la Reine
Galeries Royales St Hubert
1000 Bruxelles

Orchidée
Mariastraat 18
8000 Bruges

Ann Thys
't Apostelientje
Balstraat 11
8000 Bruges

FRANCE
Centre d'Initiations à la Dentelle du Puy
2 Rue Duguesclin
43000 Le Puy en Vela

A L'Econome
Anne-Marie Deydier
Ecole de Dentelle aux
    Fuseaux
10 rue Paul Chenavard
69001 Lyon

Rougier and Plé
13–15 Bd des Filles de
    Calvaire
75003 Paris

GERMANY
Der Fenster Laden
Berliner Str. 8
D 6483 Bad Soden
Salmünster

P. P. Hempel
Ortolanweg 34
1000 Berlin

HOLLAND
Blokker's Boektiek
Bronsteeweg 4/4a
2101 AC Heemstede

Theo Brejaart
Dordtselaan 146–148
PO Box 5199
3008 AD Rotterdam

Heikina de Rüyter
Zuiderstraat 1
9693 ER Nieweschans

Magazijn *De Vlijt*
Lijnmarkt 48
Utrecht

SWITZERLAND
Fadehax
Inh. Irene Solca
4105 Biel-Benken
Basel

NEW ZEALAND
Peter McLeavey
P.O. Box 69.007
Auckland 8

USA
Arbor House
22 Arbor Lane
Roslyn Heights
NY 11577

Baltazor Inc.
3262 Severn Avenue
Metairie
LA 7002

Beggars' Lace
P.O. Box 481223
Denver
Colo 80248

Berga Ullman Inc.
P.O. Box 918
North Adams
MA 01247

Frederick J. Fawcett
129 South Street
Boston
MA 02130

Happy Hands
3007 S. W. Marshall
Pendelton
Oreg 97180

International Old Lacers
P.O. Box 1029
Westminster
Colo 80030

The Lacemaker
23732-G Bothell Hwy, SE
Bothell
WA 98021

Lace Place de Belgique
800 S. W. 17th Street
Boca Raton
FL 33432

Lacis
3163 Adeline Street
Berkeley CA 94703

Robin's Bobbins
RT1 Box 1736
Mineral Bluff
GA 30559-9736

Robin and Russ
Handweavers
533 North Adams Street
McMinnville
Oreg 97128

Some Place
2990 Adline Street
Berkeley
CA 94703

Osma G. Todd Studio
319 Mendoza Avenue
Coral Gables
FL 33134

**The Unique And Art Lace
   Cleaners**
5926 Delman Boulevard
St Louis
MO 63112

Van Scriver Bobbin Lace
130 Cascadilla Park
Ithaca
NY 14850

The World in Stitches
82 South Street
Milford
N.H. 03055

Sources of Information

UNITED KINGDOM

The Lace Guild
The Hollies
53 Audnam
Stourbridge
West Midlands DY8 4AE

The Lacemakers' Circle
49 Wardwick
Derby DE1 1HY

The Lace Society
Linwood
Stratford Road
Oversley
Alcester
War BY9 6PG

The British College of Lace
21 Hillmorton Road
Rugby
War CV22 5DF

Ring of Tatters
Miss B. Netherwood
269 Oregon Way
Chaddesden
Derby DE2 6UR

**United Kingdom Director
   of International Old
   Lacers**
S. Hurst
4 Dollis Road
London N3 1RG

USA
International Old Lacers
Gunvor Jorgensen (Pres.)
366 Bradley Avenue
Northvale
NR 076647

Lace & Crafts magazine
3201 East Lakeshore Drive
Tallahassee
FL 32312-2034

OIDFA
(*International Bobbin and
   Needle Lace Organization*)
Kathy Kauffmann
1301 Greenwood
Wilmette
Illinois 60091

Index